Enchanted Beings

A Trip Around the Wheel of the Year
with 8 Practitioners

Jenny Chapman

Copyright

ISBN 978-0-9956188-2-4

Printed and bound in Great Britain by
TJ International Ltd, Padstow, Cornwall

Author's note

This book is based on transcripts of nine interviews conducted by the author, as well as articles, course notes, healing records, research and her own memory of events between 31st October 2015 and 2016.

Contents

For my mum
and the connection we built during my childhood illness

The Wheel of the Year

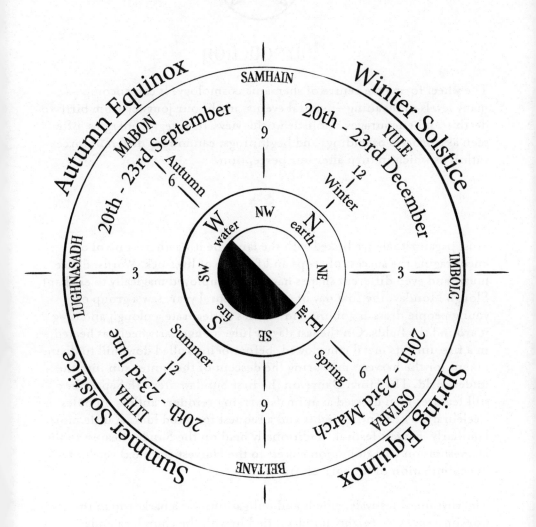

Introduction

The wheel forms the centre of shamanic cosmology. It can encompass many levels of meaning — natural events, myth, our journey from birth to death — and encourages a holistic world-view. Its integral energies, often seen as a process of endings and beginnings, can unlock different forces within us which in turn alter our perception.

Most pagan rituals are linked with the land, be it weather-control or encouraging the success of crops and fertility of livestock. Words, dance, music and even different shapes have been employed magically to enchant. Plough Monday, the first day of the agricultural year, saw a group of young people dress as goblins and witches to decorate a plough and drag it around the fields. On the last day of July, a huge cartwheel was heated in a fire until its metal rim glowed, before being rolled downhill to divine omens for the harvest, mirroring the descent of the winter sun into the underworld. The Horn Dance on the first Sunday after 4th September still features men dressed as animals carrying reindeer antlers on poles in a celebration of hunting rights and a request for good luck. A little more familiarly, harvest festival, traditionally held on the Sunday nearest to the Harvest moon (the full moon closest to the Harvest equinox) celebrates the culmination of the agricultural year.

The rhythm of festivals, rituals and obligations was a backdrop to the working year. Over eighty holidays, tied in with the church calendar, saints' days and the agricultural year, were celebrated annually. A semi-literate to literate populace did all the manual labour and, in the absence of a calendar, the rhythm of festivals meant they knew when to plant seeds, pick fruit and harvest crops. Linking people with festivals — and by extension, markets — simultaneously increased trade, promoted awareness of the time of year and marked celebrations.

While the life and work of our ancient cultures were governed by the cycles and rhythms of nature – the elements, the seasons, the movements of the moon, sun and planets – nowadays our daily lives are less ruled by such practical activities.

The Celts, incomers from the Indo-European world who incorporated their own practices with those of the indigenous Picts in northern Britain and the Formorians in Ireland, divided the year into four quarters carrying the names of our four Pagan festivals as well as the solstices and equinoxes. The meanings of twelve divisions as found in the 2nd century Gaulish calendar discovered at Coligney show that the year was divided into times when different things were done: *seed fall, darkest depths, cold-time, stay-home time, time of ice, time of winds, shoots-show, time of brightness, horse-time, claim-time, arbitration-time* and *song-time*. A further division of the year into dark and light halves also existed.

In addition to the festivals themselves, other temporal and special markers provided ways of navigating the world. Traditionally, the eight directions were used as a teaching tool, rather than simply a route finder. The Norse/ Anglo-Saxon system and the Celtic system have different associations with each direction. For example, in the Norse tradition, south-east was associated with iron, north-west with yeast, south-west with venom and north-east with salt. In the Celtic tradition, however, the south-east is linked with Beltane, concerning feeling, the south-west is linked to Lughnasadh, concerning hearing, the north-east is linked to Imbolc, concerning taste and the north-west is linked to Samhain, concerning cleansing. Each path or direction led to different encounters and was a gateway to another state of consciousness.

The four cycles of the moon (Maiden, Lover, Mother and Crone) offered the year's progress in microcosm. The Maiden represented the new moon, a creative time for new beginnings, relationships and projects. The waxing or growing moon was the Lover, a good time to perform magic and take the first steps towards a goal. The Mother or full moon was an optimal time for gaining extra power, whilst the Crone (or dark moon) was a period of banishing magic and going inwards. The most famous moon ritual, that of the sacred marriage between the King of Summer and the High Priestess, took place at Beltane. Sacred sites like Stonehenge are linked with star lore, and were used to time rituals and obligations in the Neolithic period. The arrival of a star above a stone might signal an annual sacrifice, the re-enactment of a religious play or the time to begin hunting or planting.

The wheel also represents the human growth cycle. From a child born in Yule, to the virgin youth in Imbolc, the questing youth at the Spring Equinox and the sexually active adult at Beltane, by Litha (midsummer) one is in the midst of the course of one's life and able to reflect on time past and time remaining. At Lughnasadh, a decline begins and by Mabon one gathers all that one has achieved before death arrives with Samhain.

The life of the female, the Triple Goddess (Maiden, Mother and Crone) can also be superimposed upon the wheel. Alternatively, a project cycle can be seen through its prism — potential ideas sown at Imbolc can be warmed with fire and illuminated by candlelight. The balance of light and dark at the Spring Equinox asks us to consider what we want to leave behind and what we want to keep with us. Beltane then asks us to consider how we want to fertilise what we keep. By Midsummer, our plans should be mature, and free to take flight independently.

Paganism, by which we understand a variety of indigenous non-Christian religions, did not disappear overnight 2,000 years ago. Rather, its practices and celebrations continued below the radar, conducted by the 'village dwellers' who gave it its name. Furthermore, the Church utilized the old Pagan sites and festivals to build the new faith. Take Candlemass on 2nd February — is it really so different from Imbolc's celebration of a virgin Goddess renewing herself? Likewise, Jesus's birthday falls in mid-winter, a time when the festival of Yule celebrates the return of the male force or the light.[1] In some respects, Catholic psalms and the petitions of saints and angels are forms of magic — attempts to contact a greater being in order to alter the strings of fate — though without the original witchcraft, sympathetic magic and astrology.

A way of life died with the Agricultural Revolution. The move from a hunter-gatherer lifestyle to farming obliged people to be mindful of the future and build up food reserves for times of drought, flood, storm and pestilence (though in practice this surplus was often acquired by rulers and the elite classes). Along with working the land came bigger population centres, social networks and societies held together by myths and stories.

Our current shared, imagined order has narrowed our ability to feel. Over time, in parallel with the introduction of numbers and writing, we are no longer taught to remember the shape, touch, smell, qualities and behaviour patterns of a myriad plant and animal species, or to remember the social and ancestral background of our extended family

1. *Equally, many physical sites were appropriated from pagan use and adopted for use by Christianity.*

and community. The topology of our landscape has become alien. Reprogrammed through education and our political, economic and social systems, many of us have exchanged free association and holistic thought for compartmentalization. It is a self-reinforcing cycle.

How we begin to see life more clearly depends on how we look. Some believe that nature has more of a mutually-beneficial, and yet still 'manipulative', effect on us than we realise. Indeed, the Agricultural Revolution can be seen as hugely successful from the viewpoint of wheat. Others see a freedom in allowing plants to manipulate us and do their bidding. Each species strives to evolve by using its mutable characteristics and its drive to survive and reproduce, with little or no regard for the benefit of the individual. The wheel teaches us about these natural forces which, along with the local spirits (rocks, plants and trees) of the animist system, are critical for our survival.

As the Earth needs the sun, we each require a corresponding force or teacher. In order to change, we must first establish an inner cosmology or sacred centre within to learn stillness and regard things in relation to ourselves. Like the hunter gatherers, we can then begin to see clearly in all directions and divine the inter-relationships between things at the same time as we honour the above and below (heavens and earth) and different archetypal God/Goddess-like energies. Continued internal work is essential to develop better ways of interacting with the sacred realms. Traditional practices such as journeying to the other worlds, scrying, divination (second sight), spiritual healing and poetic invocation assist. Over time we may begin to see our place in the scheme of things.

To the shaman (and the practitioners in this book) all is sacred and every action is filled with meaning. Creation should be viewed as a whole in order to see clearly. In a non-dualistic world there is no division between death and rebirth, good and evil, light and darkness, matter and spirit, outer and inner, summer and winter, masculine and feminine, mine and yours. In the shamanic worlds, creation is in harmony with the elements, the animals, the birds, the fish, the insects, the plants and mineral life forms. Here we become part of the natural world again.

In this book may be found a number of ways of listening to wise beings – be they human, plant, animal, the land or the mountains themselves. Their living teachings are designed to draw us to them and shape us. As our senses open, the boundaries between us thin. Our consciousness becomes immersed in the totality of what is around us and we communicate with all the energies and resonances of the world.

The secret to following the golden threads is immersion in the thread through the use of the feeling sense, an immersion so deep that you forget everything else but the touch of that thread and the effort to bring it into form in the world.

Stephen Buhner

We cannot explain the choices that history makes, but we can say something very important about them: history's choices are not made for the benefit of humans.

Yuval Harari

Chapter 1
Samhain - 31st October

Thou know'st the mask of night is on my face,
Else would a maiden blush bepaint my cheek
For that which thou hast heard me speak tonight.
Fain would I dwell on form. Fain, fain deny
What I have spoke. But farewell compliment!
Dost thou love me? I know thou wilt say "ay,"
And I will take thy word. Yet if thou swear'st
Thou mayst prove false. At lovers' perjuries,
They say, Jove laughs. O gentle Romeo,
If thou dost love, pronounce it faithfully.

Romeo and Juliet, William Shakespeare

Samhain is a day of remembrance, when the veil between the worlds is thinnest and communication with the dead permissible. It is a time to visit the underworld, to heal, set boundaries and seek one's inner truth.

For witches, Samhain – pronounced *sowen, soween, saw-win, saw-vane* or *shaven* – is the highest holy day and the eve of the new year. In fact, its names in other cultures are fairly well known: Hallowe'en, Feast of the Dead (*Feile na Marbh*), Day of the Dead (*Dia de los Muertos*), Ancestor Night, Apple Fest, All Saints Day, All Hallows' Eve and Martinmas. Samhain means Summer's End, and it marks the beginning and ending of the Celtic year – the close of harvest and the start of winter.

Traditionally a time of darkness and fear for the Church, it was actually one of regeneration for the Celts. This dark, formless time is an opportunity to uproot and reflect on 'stuck' energy patterns, illnesses and behaviours and to consider the mysteries and wisdom within, aligning oneself with all that needs to disintegrate. We change what we can, accept what we cannot, endure and wait in silence. Only then can new possibilities emerge.

ISLA – the Queen of Yew

Isla has been exploring indigenous traditions, ceremony, ritual and story since her childhood in Nigeria and Japan, and through her studies of History, photography and Shamanism. Her inquiry has been guided by the question: 'What gives meaning to human life'?

Spending periods of time as part of the supporting team at various meditation retreats, Isla unravelled her mind and gathered her spirit; weaving together a practice based on connecting with Nature, authenticity, expression and deep listening.

Whilst undertaking a training in shamanic healing, Isla was called to live in solitude in the ancient woodlands of Sussex, where her deepest training began, with Nature as her guide. The trees, mushrooms and plants became teachers and through her initiation with the yew tree and a pilgrimage to Islay, she was shown her purpose in life — to be a conduit for the trees and ancestral realms.

If I'm not holding a ceremony I feel I'm not marking the transitions or acknowledging the year's transformations or shifts. Every six weeks there is a Celtic festival and something in my spirit feels the need to honour it.

My favourite festival is Samhain. It's the ancestral time, when the veil is thinnest to the other realms. For me, it means a journey to the Yew trees. I might have three fires burning, and strip naked. A proper cleansing of heat and water.

Hallowe'en and Bonfire night may have usurped the pagan festivals, but they are in essence the same kind of honouring. Dressing up and trick-or-treating are about releasing inhibitions. You have a period which is a kind of no-time – anything goes. You are encouraged to express your wild and promiscuous side, whatever it is. In costume, no one knows who you are. The rest of the year you know that you have that window, so perhaps you behave more virtuously.

Samhain coincides with the Mexican Day of the Dead. Lots of cultures celebrate the dead – instead of being afraid of the darkness and shadows they actually welcome and beckon them. In England, we don't. We let them wither away. I'd sooner go to graveyards to sing to the dead, tend to the graves and make offerings. But generally, it's yew trees that I'm called to on Samhain.

The Yew is a gateway or guardian to the ancestral realm, as well as the tree of life, death and rebirth. In the Celtic lunar calendar, it's the beginning and end of all the trees – the time of transformation. It comes just before Birch, the tree of new beginnings when the New Year begins. Yew trees are often found in graveyards, which is significant. In 2012, I went on a 24-hour vision quest at the ancient King Yew in Gloucestershire. I chose to do it on the dark moon (the time when there is no solar reflection and the lunar face is in darkness) closest to Samhain.

I couldn't find the tree for ages. I set up camp and nestled in. I had some mushrooms with me and asked the tree if that was the thing to do. Then the heavens opened – lightning and thunder. After a little while I started to yawn, which often accompanies coming up on mushrooms. This time I remember every breath was a yawn. It went on for an hour and half. The action of yawning is surrendering – the movement of drawing in on the in-breath, looking at the heavens and then bowing down to the ground on the out-breath. It felt like a huge wave of healing energy from spirit down to the earth through this tree and then through me. That night was one of the most powerful experiences of my life – among the elements, in the dark, just a few feet from the perimeter of the tree. By dawn I was freezing and soaked... I remember circling the Yew tree for ages, dancing and singing to it, trying to warm myself up. Then I sat up inside it for hours. Just being with a tree like that for 24 hours is a beautiful experience. It is something I should do more often.

I guess I don't have a set way of connecting. However, I always introduce

myself first. I merge with the tree by just being with it. I don't have a visual strength but I'm quite kinesthetic – feeling is my way of seeing. If I have my back to a tree, I can feel its rhythm through my spinal fluid. Aligning with it, I can plug into something. What the tree does with its sap, its life-force, moving up, is actually quite similar to what is practised in cranial sacral therapy. Then,

Isla birthing a drum

just by being present, I see what comes and follow any idea that comes up, however mad it sounds.

The yawning experience was incredibly significant. I felt a little discombobulated, and didn't know how to integrate what had happened. I was a little confused. However, since that point I have been obsessed with the Yew tree. I devoted myself to it. The Yew is still my guardian.

In October 2012, I started visiting ancient yews around the country, using a website to find their locations.[2] Some of them had perfect hollows, and if I could, I would sleep inside them. It was Samhain at Kingly Vale in 2012 when I built a womb under a Yew tree and laid a fire. I had a drum I wanted to birth in order to gain permission to begin these tree journeys. After drumming for a long time I felt surrounded by drummers as if the ancestors were spiralling around me, almost deafening. With them around me I went from fearful at not being able to see anything around the fire to completely open and receptive. It was very much the beginning of my ancestral journey.

There were three yews within an hour of where I lived at the time, and I felt the need to take an initiation with the Yew tree's poisonous red berries.[3] The seed contains wisdom, for within a seed is the potential

2. *www.ancient-yew.org*
3. *Eating yew seeds is not recommended. They are poisonous.*

of a fully-grown tree. I started preparing to take these seeds on my 28th birthday, the return of Saturn in my birth chart signalling a completion. I made a mead with the Yew berries and took a few mouthfuls a day, building up resistance for my actual birthday. It was my first Christmas away from my family. I had never felt such a commitment to anything.

The day prior, I fasted. I spent the day in an ancient Yew forest in Sussex

Isla feeling the rhythm of a Yew tree

writing poems and collecting Yew branches and berries. That day I thought I would meet my death. I questioned whether I was going mad. There was a fear, but this was quieted by a sense of purpose and support from the tree. I had three seeds — a trinity. Down by the river was a Yew, and I built a fire and curled up in the roots. There was a full moon. I had heard that if I only swallowed the seeds, I might be okay. So I had to chew them. That was the only way to confront what I needed to confront.

The experience itself was something of a disappointment — peacefulness, a being present with my body and wishing for something to come about. I had no fear. If anything, I felt disappointed not to have had a taste of death. It was a good lesson for me to recognise that changes can be subtle. Initiations are about an end to what has been and a rebirth, and my commitment and devotion to the tree have changed my life. All is exactly as it is meant to be.

About two weeks later, I acted as my sister's birth partner. I moved in with her, and it was an intense time. I didn't know anything about pregnancy. The birth was long and I saw my sister in a new way. I held her newborn on my chest and I was unable to make sense of what was going on.

That year, I fell pregnant as well, conceiving on Halloween. I had planned a two week retreat in the woods over Samhain to call in my next initiation, not knowing I was pregnant. I realised I was, on the full moon in Birch - *Beithe* in Celtic, meaning birth. It affirmed my relationship with the Yew tree. I now feel I can meet any Yew anywhere and be recognised by it. It's like I've made some commitment, and as a result they all know me. My sister wrote a thank-you card afterwards and addressed it to the Queen of Yew. I remember reading it and thinking, 'Yes, look at you!'

Artificial womb by Cadbury hill fort

At Imbolc 2017, I visited a large artificial womb by Cadbury hill fort.

Someone has etched the words *Crows' Castle* outside it, and it is clearly used as a sacred space. There is a broom inside.

I had been up there with a friend before, and I kept being called back. I didn't know my intention, exactly. I had a few mushrooms, and felt that I wanted to connect to them. Towards dusk, I drank some mushroom tea and went and lay in the womb, drumming for a little bit and then just cried my eyes out. I felt like I revisited my childhood — a lot of painful memories and grief, as well as the grief of the land there. I assume it has a bloody history. Just a deep release of grief. It felt so good. I could see it was dark outside and slightly raining and I had prepared a fire. So I went out and lit it. I felt so grateful for the energy, the life force, of this roaring fire. I could feel it within, almost but not quite ready to burst.

Then I put on my headphones and let rip with my staff, stomping around the woods. I tried to awaken something in my sacral chakra (the second chakra, associated with the emotional body, sensuality and creativity). I could really feel this heat and the stirring of something. I allowed myself to feel free and uninhibited. It had been a while. The rain was really elemental. Just delicious.

I see myself as a tree lady. My sister used to make dresses with long trains. I have a photo of myself ten years ago beside an upright cracked piece of oak. The oak is a doorway.

It's interesting how things weave together.

There is definitely work to do with the trees this year.

Isla sitting on a dead Oak tree

This Longing

What is this flame
That beckons me —
Deep within the forest,
Hidden inside the trees?

This burning yearning
That calls to me
From the silence
Of the full moon.

My thirst cannot be quenched
By false idols.
For only Yew, my love,
Only Yew can fill me.

What is this vision
That beguiles me
Of a forgotten treasure
Cast in darkness?

This map of hidden roots
That guides me
Beyond the veil
Into your arms.

My love cannot be met
By shimmering masks.
For only Yew, my love,
Only Yew can see me.

What is this dream
That awakens me
To hear the beating heart
Of mother's womb?

This primal rhythm
That dances me
Into sweet ecstasy
Beneath your shade.

My song cannot be heard
By deaf ears.
For only Yew, my love,
Only you can hear my longing.

Chapter 2
Yule – 21ˢᵗ December

A daughter
is birthed by the Sun goddess
after she is swallowed by the wolf
and shall ride
as the gods are dying
the old paths of her mother.

VafÞrúðnismál, the third poem in the Poetic Edda

Yule, the winter solstice or 'dark night of our souls' marks the shortest day of the year. It is a time when one cycle of the wheel ends and a new one begins. Winter provides time for deep shadow work when we deal with our primitive human emotions and impulses driven by our ego consciousness. We enter a period of death and inner transformation in preparation for a rebirth. Eventually we meet the shame, paralysis, blocks and inhibitions locked into our body.

This is the time when the Crone or wise woman is reborn again as a Maiden. 'She who cuts the thread' or 'Our lady in darkness' calls back the Sun God. At the same time, this dark aspect of the Goddess is in the process of giving birth. At New Year's we make resolutions which release us from the unconscious drives of childhood traumas and past lives. First, we must step beyond the bounds of rational thought into the realms of feeling, intuition and dreams.

TIM – Rune Master

Tim is a practitioner of Northern European shamanism (Celtic, Norse, Anglo-Saxon shamanic practice), Utta sitting (sitting on the land to commune with Spirit) and a renowned shaman and bard.

He is clairvoyant, a Master in the arts of healing and magic and a boxer.

Raised in Somerset from Welsh heritage he spent much of his youth out on the land undertaking ceremonies and building a relationship with the spirits.

Based in Glastonbury, Tim is a familiar face and regarded as an exquisite storyteller, harpist and rune diviner.

My job is to serve. I do whatever I am told by Spirit. The spiritual and healing work comes first, and afterwards I can fit in other mundane things such as finances. A lot of people are stuck in their *Orlog*, their 'place of goings on' where things happen, since they haven't worked the magic and released things in their past. Even though they are probably unaware of it, their shadows linger like poison because they haven't faced them. It is a miserable existence reliving the same old experiences or patterns. You can't go in and deal with them all at once as that would lead to a break in the psyche. Rather, the work needs to be done systematically, bit by bit and at the right time. You have to ask the appropriate questions and to be guided by Spirit. It needs a gradual release until you get to the nub of the problem. That way you are working with nature, not against it.

The Norse practice of *Seidr* enables you to journey into the spirit world. As your guide into these worlds I give instructions, sing and play the drum and sometimes the harp whilst you journey. Imagine me singing the words *Yara, yara, yara...* to a rhythmic drum-beat as you relax into a shamanic trance. It is the time of year of Yule and the winter solstice. There are frosts, cold winds and darkness. You see a pathway and take in the landscape. It is very cold. This is the place where you review and are open to what needs to be let go: hopes and dreams that did not grow well for you and habits that need to be given away, where you have planted seeds of endeavour in a wrong direction. Things at the end of their cycle which need to be put aside or released. Beside the fire are gifts. One of these gifts is a golden sickle. Take it into your hand. It is yours. With this sickle you can choose to cut the cords (to the past) and let go with dignity. Be open to what you are shown. It could be attitudes or behaviours as well as goals or dreams. If you are not ready to do these things you just say so. Everything has its right timing – that is what this journey is about. For you to recognise this. Be open to any help or helpers.

Now the darkness starts to break and the sun starts to rise. You see a golden bristled boar.[4] The God Freyr's boar. An eagle flies close to the sun. It is a time of new beginnings and the end of the darkness. A new season. Now this rising light lets you be open to any new year's resolutions and long term goals. Changes will be slow and peaceful, steady. You will receive solutions. These are the sparks of *Muspelheim* where the destructive and creative fires of the underworld dwell. You may receive gifts or be shown other things. Know that you can always return to this place. See how the landscape has changed. Freyr's Yule boar brings the light. As the sun rises and waxes so will your endeavours. Peace comes with correct timing

4. *In German paganism, the boar was sacrificed as part of the Yule celebration. There was a tradition of making solemn vows by laying hands on its bristles and swearing an oath.*

and correct efforts and working with natural cycles of the Earth. Know that the tide has now turned.

The runes are a tool which will help you understand yourself and the spirit world. Runic energies connect with everything within us. The winter runes are Hagalaz (a period of disruption), Isa (stasis) and Jara (gradual change). Jara, associated with the Yule festival which is the winter solstice, follows after the ice of Isa. Its colours are red and green like those used at Christmas, its gift a golden sickle and its animals the Eagle and the Yule boar. This rune rules *Midgard* or middle earth and the waking consciousness or the ego consciousness. Trees linked with it are the Oak (with its regal powers and access to ethereal planes) and the Holly (the Sword of Truth). The symbol carved on the rune face represents one half of the year as darkness and the other half, light. Both are needed to make the whole.

Scyld, a hero of the Anglo-Saxon epic, and Freyr (Lord) are Gods associated with Jara. An ancient Anglo-Saxon poem concerning Jara energy reads:

> Summer is called joyful, when God lets
>
> Holy heaven's King / shining fruits,
>
> Be born from Earth for rich or poor.

As you can see, this rune brings the return of the light and all things that are fruitful. In the mythology Freyr is the ruler of peace, wealth, fertility, rain and sunshine. He lives in the homeland of the elves or the realms of our higher consciousness. He rides *Gullinbursti* (Golden-Bristled) a boar and owns the ship *Skíðblaðnir* which always has a favourable breeze. In the legends, he falls in love with a female giantess but first has to give away his magic sword[5], which fights on its own, and slay a giant with an antler[6] to win her as his wife.

 Jara brings gentle change. It is great for farmers, herbalists and all those who work with the Earth (and the medicine wheel). If Jara is someone's personal power rune they will have skills in those areas. They will work with the plants and fauna but their medium will be the medicine wheel – informing how you work at different times of the year and which Gods relate and can help. This rune is about timing and fertility. When cast

5. *Metaphysically the sword represents discrimination and the penetrating power of the intellect.*

6. *The deer is a symbol of spiritual authority in some cultures. Antlers, like a crown, are considered to be above the body and, as such, closer to the sky and sacred.*

upright, it grows anything in a gentle way. It won't shake your foundations. Growth is in its own season and to be cultivated. It is about understanding the seasons and cycles of all situations. Also about karma, returns, completion and attainment.

The runes are a tool to access the spirit world and to ready someone for deeper work. Each rune is part of the initiate's journey, helping to gain medicine and strength in order to reach the next level psychologically, mentally, spiritually and physically. A journeying phase is associated with each, along with the medicine that needs to be accrued before you can proceed to, and understand, the next stage. The nine worlds of the Norse world tree are, of essence, a different, deeper layer of consciousness. Spirit worlds should not be accessed before you are ready. It is a bit like boxing – a beginner should never enter the ring with someone completely out of their league. In one way, it is possible to look at the rune realms as yourself. There are some parts of ourselves we are not ready to go to. If you try to access a part of your soul that is not ready, an animal guardian – for example, a wolf or a dragon – may be really aggressive towards you. They won't let you go there. They protect you.

Sometimes you can come up against trickster or evil spirits. When that happens I sing the *Galder* and raise my protection. If you study Norse mythology, names are important and contain secrets. Their translations denote certain God or Goddess functions, and the poetic kennings will mean something like 'giver'. It is important for your understanding of what is being said. If you call upon Odin under his name 'All Father' it means 'the Great Spirit' but *Grimnir* is him with a hood or a cloak which represents stealth and not being able to be seen. *Gangleri* is his wanderer aspect. As in your dreams, it is important to distinguish between good and bad spirits and to stop going down a route you shouldn't be on.

In the period of the dark we need to review our year and what has happened, in particular the things that did not grow or are not growing and need to be put aside. Then we must think about our New Year's resolutions because that is what it is really about. The dark things need to be accessed and let go. Some are frozen and need to thaw whilst other experiences would benefit from being forgotten. You have learned what is needed. If something is not working then the harvest might not have been good on the karmic, physical, mental, spiritual and emotional levels. As you move from the depths of winter it becomes time for the ice to melt. The wheel turns from the cold weather into the summer solstice. The season starts to turn.

The Jara rune concerns time. At the winter solstice, the sun stands still. A new year and a new cycle begin with the rising of the sun. However, before joy and hope can return, you are in the dark. You need to look at your year, your cycle. This is why we have Christmas and New Year's celebrations. It all comes from our Anglo-Saxon and Norse traditions. However, while Christians promote Yule as a very happy time, in the old traditions there is an old spirit called the Grampus that needs to be banished to enable the return of the sun.

The Welsh traditions of Taliesin contain the tale of Morfran, whose name means 'utter darkness,' which would be at the time of Yule. There is nothing good about him, he had a bad heart and was a nasty individual. Born a twin, his sister Creirwy was beautiful and everything fair, whilst Morfran was everything that is utterly despicable. A magic brew was made by Ceridwen, their mother and the Celtic Goddess of rebirth, transformation and inspiration, in order to make him at least wise, even if his appearance was horrible and behaviour awful. This ignorance and darkness are the things that we need to let go.

In the rune realms, you have a chance to be shown the things that might need to be released. With the right protocol, on the right day, at the right time for you with the right type of medicine and the gateways open, you will obtain a deep understanding and a letting go. If I have put my efforts into a project that is falling on infertile ground, and my efforts go unrewarded, I release the things that are blocking me from success. My life begins to change as the return of the light commences. At the New Year, I look at resolutions — things that I would like to grow or plant, long-term projects. I swear an oath. That is where the *sonar-blót* rite comes from — a New Year's resolution. The Yule festival deals with the melting of the ice and the return of the light. It is a time to be set free.

Chapter 3
Imbolc – 1st / 2nd February

Rosy is the west,
Rosy is the south,
Rosy are her cheeks,
And a rose her mouth.

Maud, Tennyson

Imbolc is the time of year when trees come into leaf, flowers blossom and birds sing. The earth awakens from its long winter sleep and the agricultural year commences. Our generative force returns and a spark of intuition comes from within.

Imbolc – pronounced 'ee-molc' – is one of the four Celtic fire festivals, and marks the time when the Goddess changes from Crone to Maiden. The Christian representation of Brigid as St Bride or St Bridget completely reverses the festival's original concern with the raising of sexual energies. Now it is known as the 'Purification of the Virgin Mary.'

St Bride's Day is traditionally connected with the stirrings from hibernation of the adder and viper, both fertility symbols and signs of renewal. It is also represented by the rowan and willow trees whose energy helps things move from the unconscious to the conscious level.

FOREST – a Land Spirit

Forest has a love of nature, the wide outdoors and adventure. Her early work-history was practical, and linked to the land, as a carpenter and as a heavy goods vehicle driver. Subsequently she has studied the Druidic path, holds a Masters in Shamanic practice and is a practitioner of Inca energy medicine.

Forest enjoys the support of a number of spiritual elders and is a speaker and teacher in her own right. She has travelled the world, including the Americas.

Forest's diagnosis of high functioning Autism, ADHD and developmental PTSD has focused her shamanic practice on the ways of 'the Wounded Healer' and trauma support and care. She is currently seeking a dry cave (for a meditation retreat) and further shamanic adventures.

When I was younger and lived on the farm near North End (around Batheaston) I felt I could smell the wind and detect a change in temperature or pressure. There was a horseshoe of valleys and I had an intimate knowledge of the weather in each one. I walked every inch of that area — there wasn't a valley, a stream or river that I didn't explore thoroughly. Early in the year around Imbolc there came a wind like a kiss. It was this 'sweet wind' which announced Spring time. It would be really warm for one day, one morning or afternoon. This happened three times and then it would stay.

Weather work is purely instinctive for me. I am a tympanic synaesthete — meaning I feel vibration all the time, be it from people or the environment. It's like I'm a snare drum in the corner. I can also see wavelength and perceive people's energy. I have an acute sense of smell. We are all naturally synaesthetic. In traditional aboriginal culture, all the senses operate in an amplified manner — coherently, interchangeably and eloquently. We all possess that basic ability. A first nation elder once said, 'Our people were healthy until we drank the town water.' The water and land have become denuded of the information that comes from the Earth. Fluoride in the toothpaste, aspartane in the food and chlorine in the water dull our perceptions.

The plants appear not to talk to us at this current time because we don't know how to listen. Whilst the solstices and equinoxes are firmly fixed by calendar date, quarter festivals such as Imbolc and Beltane follow the arrival of plants. If a particular plant shows its face, or blossoms, that is the signal for these celebrations to start. Nowadays, we find it more difficult to detect such subtle changes.

In the same way that we have distinct personalities, each area has its own smell, nature and — often — weather. Everything has its own energy signature. The sound of water changes after it has rained a lot. In Robert Graves's *The White Goddess* different winds make the trees speak in different ways. It used to be the case that I could drink ground water and tell which individual plants had been there. Western progress has impeded that ability for me. The increased bacteria in the gut of people who live off the land is actually part of a communication with the land which we in the West no longer have.

The present system deprives us of a lot of diversity. Our rivers are empty when they had once been full, our springs are dead and dried up and the ground water has been robbed so repeatedly that the natural bodies of water have been challenged. When I first went out into the world there wasn't as much pollution, population or sensory overload as there is now. Some things only live in my memory. I remember when there was only the rare car and the majority of people walked or cycled places. People didn't have lots of radios, and music came from a small range of sources – the band down the pub or a mate who played guitar. An all-pervasive homogenisation wasn't yet in existence. Rebellion or difference was still natural. Now there is a perception that we are under threat. We are afraid of each other.

I was a very disturbed, distressed, unhappy young woman and spent a lot of time on my own. Out walking on the land I started to get an inner reply from what I have since come to understand as the spirit beings in the area – the grass, the trees. Pouring out my woes eventually became a conversation. I would be going along a path and divine 'Go left!' I had nothing better to do, so I obeyed. This became so innate that when I later became a truck driver in Kent, I used to rely on a kind of internal sat nav. Post codes didn't exist at the time. Since then, I've read about Aboriginals in Australia who had some kind of a compass in their noses which informed them which direction north was in. They had a natural sense of direction. They knew how to detect and determine, with their awareness of the environment, when the yin[7] water energies were going to arise and come to the surface on their dream or song lines. We still have traditions in this country which are similar barometers of our seasonal movements.

Weather shamanism is a relationship, in the way that a dance is a relationship. I connect through sound and dance. A spirit language. It's not one where you can say 'That word means *ball*' and 'That word means *orange.*' It's an energetic language, so one sound can mean a lot, or a lot of sounds can mean very little. Now I'm aware of the translation as I get the pictures in my head. I also get the words. I understand the energy essence. It's like a spirit song which will accomplish certain deeds. I use and trust this language. It says in spirit what I don't always know how to say. If someone came to me and said we've had a terrible drought in our village I would say, 'I will come and see what I can do.'

I'm really aware it only takes two generations to lose the land knowledge that you have when you live on and with the land. I keep hold of it as if it is the most valuable piece of cloth I've ever owned. Since my residency in Shamanka (a school offering training in the healing and shamanic arts) four or five years ago, I've been building my library: how to forage, my divination cards, notes on hen keeping, bee keeping, sheep keeping; all my Inca library. Some of the books – like Zachariah Hitchin and Elizabeth

---

7. *Yin, as opposed to Yang water is characterised by its ability to change shape and characteristics. It is represented in nature by rain, clouds, mist etc.*

Jenkins — have been recommended to me. They write about space, quantum physics, the space-time continuum and ancient knowledge. Ideally, before I die I would gather a group of young people together and pass this knowledge on.

The books remind me of the knowledge I used to claim as my own. When I left my family home as a toddling child the first place I went to was a family farm. Later, I stood among people with generational knowledge. Their family employed the old remedies. So when the sick Spring calves which had been born after Imbolc around the Equinox started scouring I used to clean the byre, whitewash the walls, put hydrated lime in the lower level bed and create an extra layer to make it super clean. If they were already in a deep layer bed we didn't dig it out, so as to preserve the heat. One of them would make up a potion of arrowroot and other herbs to bind the gut and stop them from scouring. Oregano oil is anti-microbial and anti-bacterial — you can use it like an antibiotic for some things. It is similar to grapefruit seed oil, and has citric properties.

Later, when I had no home and was living off the kindness and good graces of other people I would return to my love of farming. My dream has always been to have 25 acres. I would like the outbuildings to do something shamanic with. I miss the animals, the cows and the sounds they make. At the end of March when the wind changes, they used to stamp at the gate because they could smell the grass growing. In the barn they keened for the land until they were let out to pasture.

All my life I have stamped my feet and yearned for such a release. Imbolc is a time of preparation and in the wheel of the year it is when the last phase before birth called 'kick in the womb time' is played out. An Australian 'jobbing shaman' Patrick MacManaway took me around the wheel of the year in this different way and through his work I became aware that a healing relating to this time of the year and its opposite side of the wheel, Lughnasadh (where rewards are handed out), was required. Later, I entered the underworld of the Druid King to look at this dark and deeply damaged side of me. I experienced something similar to mycelium's relationship to both a seed and the earth, as my shadow side went down into the darkness to communicate underground with my unconscious.

It was with the order of Bards, Ovates and Druids that I gained a familiarity with ancient Celtic stories such as those of Taliesin, and my relationship with the land was renewed. At White Horse Druid camp this year I used a teaching model around birthing a child, knitted into three days of journeying. It brought up deep things for people. Meanwhile, I felt my mother's pain and frustration after a medical issue gave her problems breast feeding. I do not have children but realised this archetypal inheritance had also fashioned me. Releasing this monstrous energy enabled me to feel compassion for women and the demands placed upon them, and an enormous appreciation for my mother who had done her best with a lack of support. The voice of my story is not pretty but its power eventually allowed me to enter and move with ease around the whole wheel of the year and in doing so to speak of – and experience – joy.

We need to maintain the knowledge of how to live with and on the land and to cooperate with the animals at a sustainable, natural and gentle level. There is a point – or a scale – at which you detach from being close to your food source. In the West, we no longer know what it is like to garner our own food as a community experience.

When I was flint-napping recently, I was reminded of foraging. To nap is to strike and remove a piece of stone that can then be used purposefully to make a tool. I learned the sounds that the tools should make, how to hold them and how they are struck. 'What do those plants look like? Where do you find them? Do they look different at different times of year?' It is a similar connection. I'm currently teaching myself foraging for wild food and their medicine. I've got a beautiful cabinet full of tinctures and oils. I hope before I breathe my last I will be able to wander in nature and the plants will speak to me and that I won't need the books. They will tell me who and what they are. I hope to be in a context where that relationship is necessary and has the space to be.

Chapter 4
Ostara – 21st / 22nd March

It was a lover and his lass,
  With a hey, and a ho, and a hey nonino,
That o'er the green corn-field did pass,
  In spring time, the only pretty ring time,
When birds do sing, hey ding a ding, ding,
  Sweet lovers love the spring.

As You Like It, William Shakespeare

Ostara, which falls at the vernal or Spring Equinox, is a time of fertility represented by a beguiling maiden with a basket of eggs. She brings new life and rebirth and her union with Herne the Hunter releases repressed instincts.

It is a time of equilibrium – to balance dark and light, inner and outer, unconscious and conscious and the intuitive and rational mind. The old rule is overthrown, and new ideas are manifested in order to move forward with new understanding.

As the dragon energies awaken within the Earth, oestrogen stimulates ovulation in mammals, and seeds begin to germinate and sprout. In many rural communities, these two days are regarded as the official beginning of Spring.

ELIANA – Healing Hands

Eliana is known as a gifted Shamanka, Medicine Woman and Healer. She has trained for over 30 years with a number of shamans and medicine people from different indigenous traditions. Exploring the Inca tradition has become a personal compulsion.

Eliana is dedicated to teaching women the mysteries of the path of the female shaman. She is considered a leading teacher of women's Shamanism and the recovering of the Feminine Principle.

Eliana is the founder of the **Shamanka, Traditional School of Women's Shamanism** *which offers training in the healing and shamanic arts.*

Hands are a way of receiving information. They pick up vibratory frequencies. A friend of mine was massaging a client's spine when she asked, 'Why didn't you tell me you had injured yourself when you were ten?' For years, this man had ignored the pain he had been in as a result of childhood injury to his coccyx. The information transferred itself directly through her hands to her intuitive self.

My father was an osteopath and he had healing hands — he had 'the sight.' He could focus his gaze until it became like a tunnel of light and he could see inside the body. When a client walked in the door he didn't even have to question them to know what was wrong.

We've all got gifts of some kind, even if it is simply a kindly, friendly attitude. As a child, to escape the intense atmosphere at home I used to go down a little lane and across the main road and into the wilds to sit by the river and meditate. I didn't realise what I was doing at the time. It calmed my nervous system to give myself to the water. Across the hills was a lovely beech wood. I used to fit myself into the shape of the hills and become part of the Earth. Nature was rescuing me. I have a particular affinity with the land, stones and trees.

Grandmother Twyea Niche of the Seneca tribe told me that stones are nature's brain cells, holding centuries of knowledge. They might not be as dynamically lively as crystals, but they have a deep resonance. I don't need a pendulum — I can simply pick up a stone and tell if it has an affinity with me. Does it feel friendly or not? With people, it doesn't quite work that way. I can feel if a chakra is disturbed, for example. It just doesn't feel right. I pick up negative energy like unpleasant cramps or tingles in my hands. Temperature change can also be a guide. You can't pre-program yourself, you just have to work and discover your own way.

The chakra systems come from India and the Incas. Each country has a chakra system, along with Ley lines which cross the Earth in a similar way to acupuncture lines. Usually they can be seen as light or energy. An American I once trained with could see acupuncture points. It was just ordinary for him. I am a feeler though, and my intuition is touch. I can press my palm to a tree and tell if it is happy, or whether the sap is slowing for winter. In Chinese medicine, acupuncture points actually call out to the practitioner. I can find a liver point, say, because as I reach it there is a little dip and an energetic reaction. So I press, massage it and see what it wants.

I have a range of what I call my sacred tools and – acknowledging that every substance has its own form of consciousness – I ask which would like to be involved in my work. Being living energies, stones will bring up certain emotions and it requires letting go of one's ego and intellect to listen to the voices of the things I am working with. A while back, I was a fire-keeper at a sweat lodge. There was a pit in the middle, and twelve or more stones would be brought in and water poured on. It was extremely hot. I was having real trouble getting the stones to the right heat, and determining which stones to bring in until I realised that I was looking at it from the wrong perspective. I needed to ask the stones which ones wanted to go in next. After that it was very easy.

At Shamanka, we work mainly with women. Many are disempowered and have been either physically or mentally abused. You could say they live in an almost permanent Winter, when hunting is difficult, and it isn't warm enough to plant; and so to survive they have had to learn to conserve their food and energy. Like the Spring festival of Ostara, their time with us marks a time of renewal and regeneration after this bleak period, and a return of hope and freshness. We place red on the ceremonial altar to represent the return of the Spring, warmth and fire which restores everything to life. It is a celebration of the battle between death and new life and its happy outcome. Green represents the greening of the earth. Candles represent light and fire. Water represents fertility and nourishment.

Ostara embodies new beginnings and ways of doing things. This time of year talks to a woman's inner authority. Many times I have seen women make major life-shifts, reclaiming self-worth and daring to follow a longed-for path. To their surprise, embodiment of an inner truth often resolves their fertility issues or relationship problems. Distorted relationships – how they had been living their lives and dealing with any setbacks – had been affected by their past wounding. Buried pain and trauma surface and are dealt with. In the shamanic training we encourage women to enter a dialogue with the deep psyche. They speak to their unconscious in the language of myth and symbols, combined with ritual action and ceremony. This has the effect of releasing the trapped energy around the trauma and changing the imbalanced imprint initially at an energetic level. True change comes from within.

Womb work is part of 'the work of the magical woman' or 'the cauldron of mysteries'. Women's unique ability to see the 'within' of events, situations or people is symbolised by their most treasured possession – their wombs. To utilise this gift they access deep intuitive perception helped by several archaic, magical, healing symbols. These interrelated images symbolise the powers of the sacred womb. In the pagan or wiccan traditions these are: the chalice, goblet or cauldron which represents the 'vessel' or the womb itself; the ceremonial wine, mead or 'water' contained within the vessel; ceremonial fire or candles which become the 'flame' or inner fire or spirit; a ceremonial dagger (*athame*), sword or 'knife' which is used for protection; and a 'phallus', which is the male principle within the female. This is represented by a wand or upright crystal.

The state of each woman's womb is represented by a clay pot which they create. They often have issues with menstrual blood and the time when their fertility ceases. A woman may need to re-live assaults and dishonouring or to gradually travel back through their growing up from girl-child through to womanhood. Pain and anger are woven into the pot, then silently released with forgiveness into a local stream. 'Water' – liquid, ceremonial wine, mead or particularly blood – carry potency and lineages and symbolise the 'waters of life', the creative potential, the mysteries. On their return they create a new womb pot of beauty and strength. It needs to be whole, vibrant and responsive. Empowered, they are able to create and contain life and new ideas and concepts. They bubble with energy and potential. This water-tight container prevents energy draining away and allows potent feminine powers to be reclaimed. From our wombs we access or 'birth' all potentiality from the void, the womb of creation itself.

Jumping over a sacred fire is a way of gathering fire energy or an inner fire or spirit. Four sticks must be placed in the four directions. I usually offer tobacco as a blessing, while corn gives thanks to the spirit of the fire. I might also sprinkle a few drops of essential oil into the flames. Anything that needs to be consumed by the fire – such as old or finished-with items – can be offered through a stick wrapped colourfully in wool, one wrap for each thing I want to let go of. I then ask the fire to consume it. In a group setting, someone stands behind to protect you until everything is burned. After this, the fire changes quality and becomes friendly. The shapes of the flames change, so you can kneel in front of the fire and pass your hands through, gathering the energy and putting it into your energy centres.

At Shamanka we look for our power tools after we have given them away or they have been taken from us. The knife represents that part of ourselves which will defend anything vulnerable or innocent, including our children. Some people turn the knife on themselves, which is why they are always putting themselves down and apologising – or even self-harming. We can use our knives rather like daggers. Our tongues are our knives.

The entrance to the Neolithic long barrow at Wayland's Smithy

Part of the womb work is to find our sacred knife. This entails a journey to Wayland's Smithy along an ancient track which is part of the Ridgeway. It is sited on a hill as you approach, and you can see the smoke rising and hear the clang of his hammer. It is at a crossing of two major Ley lines on a slight hill with standing stones at the entrance to a cave or long earth burrow and a grove or circle of trees around the edge. There is a most magical feel about it.

This is a ritualistic encounter in which you must ask the smith to forge your sacred dagger or sword. These have to be both portable and invisible. There is a sense as you climb the hill that you are nearing something magical and mysterious which will leave you transformed.

As you approach, you can feel the grass beneath your feet and the effort of climbing the slope. Ancient oaks line the crest of the hill and there is a circle of stone walls surrounding a low stone building. At the doorway you can sense the presence of the guardian, who asks why you have come. You must then request permission to enter. The smith is enormously tall and broad and full of power and potency, and he is expecting you. He stops and faces you with his great hammer in the air. 'Why have you come?' His eyes are piercing. They bore through you. With a certain amount of nervousness you must explain your intention. 'I have come to find my spirit dagger or knife because I wish to use this properly as a fully-empowered woman.' 'Are you sure?' he asks. 'It is a great amount of responsibility and will surely turn upon you if you misuse it.' You can feel the heat.

As you move forward it is possible to see that he is plunging a huge warrior's sword into a bucket of water. Steam rises. This is part of the tempering of the instrument. Fire and water are part of the alchemy. You must stand to one side and pay close attention to everything you see and try to understand its meaning. The smith will look at you again and go to his metals of different kinds – all placed on shelves and hanging from beams. He will choose a piece of metal for you.

Thankfully it is not too long. He holds it out. You touch it. It feels cold and strange. It is difficult to tell whether it is steel or iron, but somehow it already feels part of you. You hand the metal back to him. The smith then puts it in the fire where it begins to glow. He takes it out and hammers it on his anvil. The clanging is incessant as he beats your dagger into shape. His apprentice pumps the bellows to keep the fire hot. Five times he forges your dagger. You can see it taking shape. It is hard to understand how such a huge instrument as an anvil can make something so delicate. This time you are not permitted to look. He forges again. The sound has a different quality. It has an energy, like music. Finally, he stops. The smith plunges your dagger into water.

He places the dagger into your hands. When you look at this blade with your inner eye, strange symbols will appear in a shimmering blue light. From time to time you will see them. They may change when you change. Then the smith asks where you are going to wear it, and you have to ask the dagger where it wants to live. As you place it in a small scabbard, you begin to feel taller and stronger. There is more of you. You now owe something to the great smith. You bow to him and he salutes you. 'You have earned this. Now go.' Out of his forge, round and round, you return a different way. The guardians salute you as you walk away in full heart, aware that there is another part of you which has been re-forged as you make your way back to a different reality.

In the next area of work, the women create a phallus out of clay which can bring up powerful experiences for them. After any required deep healing and forgiveness they vigorously return the phallus to formless clay – then they take an often hilarious walk when they visualise being equipped with 'male tackle' and swagger and talk in a clichéd male fashion and on return become 'new men'. In women the divine masculine and masculine principle are represented by the 'phallus'. As a vertical symbol of proactive male energy it complements the circular integrative movement of the feminine.

On an individual scale, womb work is similar to my work with stones, crystals and Ley line energy which was originally used for ceremonies, earth healing and linking to the cosmos. From my perspective, stone circles are like energy batteries, and comprise alternate male and female stones. As people carried out ceremonies in which they processed around the stones, in and out, they would charge them up like a battery. That's how they created the energy. It's like an alternator.

In Carnac, France, rather than circles there are long lines of stones called alignments. Over time the system has become dysfunctional since some of the stones have shifted or fallen. I brought crystals with me to work with the energies and form an energetic grid. I pushed into the thorn hedge beside a great King Stone and talked to it – 'I'm sorry you are out of place.' Then I backed out. I could feel where I had to put the crystals down to draw the energy of the stone back into position. It was just within the hedge. I was calling the energy of the King Stone so it could resonate and do its job.

I've felt similar energy in other places. Don Juan Nunez Del Prado is a mystic seer and healer who works with the three masters he trained with. Each of them can trace their lineage back to the Incas. Early on in the training, Don Juan said he was going to give each of us 'the three lineages.' That means he was going to download all the wisdom and the knowledge of the three masters in one go. He put his hands upon my head and I felt the same feeling – like a battery being charged. I thought I was going to explode. He looked round at us and asked us how we each were. I heard a little voice come out of me, 'I can't move.' My senior teacher at Shamanka rushed up to help me but Don Juan told her to leave me alone as I could integrate it myself. I was hitched up by the arms to help me stand upright.

Sometimes, when I'm giving transmissions to the Shamanka women, the energy in my hands is so strong that I can barely contain it. I ask the masters to help me. Once, when I was meditating at home, I suddenly felt energy climb my spine and found myself able to call on Don Manuel Quispe. Just like him I was laughing and rocking backwards and forwards. Then I felt his energy flow through my arms and hands. I connect with his energy and am able to pass it on.

Chapter 5
Beltane – 30th April / 1st May

"Betide me weal, betide me woe,
That weird shall never daunton me;"
Syne he has kiss'd her rosy lips,
All underneath the Eildon Tree.

"Now, ye maun go wi' me," she said;
"True Thomas, ye maun go wi' me;
And ye maun serve me seven years,
Thro' weal or woe as may chance to be."

She mounted on her milk-white steed;
She's ta'en true Thomas up behind;
And aye, whene'er her bridle rung,
The steed flew swifter than the wind.

Oh they rade on, and farther on;
The steed gaed swifter than the wind;
Until they reach'd a desert wide,
And living land was left behind.

Thomas the Rhymer

Beltane celebrates the union of masculine and feminine creative energies. A Maypole is erected, crowned with a ring of fertile Goddess flowers and fastened with multi-coloured ribbons. However, Beltane is not merely marked by sexual union. Equally, a prayer also joins the God and Goddess together to make the Godhood.

This is a magical time when the Faery world awakens from slumber, and nature bursts forth in abundance. Observers should surrender to the wild instinctive forces and creative energies within them, and honour the life-force inside and outside that is greater than their own selves.

Beltane is traditionally a time to bring forth new ideas and for hopes and dreams to blossom.

DAVID — Hedge Rider

Rather than a pagan, I see myself as the product of a number of different traditions and my own unique work.

My first mystical experiences began as a child. I spent a lot of time with witches and druids as an adolescent. In one of the fields where I lived, there was a hole in the hedge that had obviously been there for a few hundred years. I heard a voice calling my name from the hedge and, thinking someone was pulling my leg, I went and looked. There was no one there. I told myself that it had to be someone who knew me from school. Next time it happened, my dogs were with me and they heard the voice, too. Quite soon afterwards, I bought a book on Celtic shamanism by John Matthews with my pocket money, and started to meditate on this gap in the hedge. It is really what started off this whole journey.

Years later I learned about hedge riding, and discovered that witchcraft was the ability to merge with the land and the trees. I used to sit with my back to the Oak trees and go into them. I could sense their roots and branches and take information from them. Hedge riding is found in north western European magic. Rae Beth, in her book on elf magic called *Green Hedgewitch*, talks about a technique whereby you stand between two trees or a gap in a hedge — a liminal space, neither one space nor another. A friend of mine could do it with one foot inside a door and the other out. You are neither here nor there and put yourself into an altered state of consciousness, entering Faery, a different state in which you can divine things that you need to know or sense, creating distance or calling spirits to you.

Within each landscape there is a spirit or focal point which allows interaction between the people and the place. The Earth retains memories just as our subconscious does. It has choices and as a living being has chosen its purpose. In Beltane 2016, we practised a form of hedge riding, but we used a whole hill. Lullover Hill can be interpreted as 'Lol Lover' — the reclining lover — and it was there that I talked to its spirits and aligned the quarters of the hill to individual stars. There were different symbols — the chalice in the West, the sword in the East, the altar in the North and the staff or flaming arrow in the South — and I assigned them different angelic beings which came naturally. By singing to them I could get them to move the space slightly out of this reality. All it takes to read the land's frequency is lying down and closing your eyes and seeing what comes into your mind.

Sometimes, travelling between the worlds gives us information about what the elves might need for us to maintain our friendship with them, or to divine what is needed to cast any particular spell. Or we may simply do it to go exploring or to develop magical skill. To go between the worlds is to travel in spirit, in most instances. Your body does not normally leave middle earth — but there have been famous cases such as Thomas the Rhymer, a 13th century Scot, whose physical journey was taken right into

Lullover Hill looking towards Glastonbury Tor

the Faery dimension of the Earth – the underworld, the other world. Sometimes fairies have come to live here in everyday human reality. The case of the green children who wandered into a Suffolk village is thought to be one such case. Folk law recounts many others.[8]

In times gone by, magic was a way of solving problems. If you lost your coat, divination could help you to find it; if someone was stealing your chickens you could find out who or cast a spell to stop them. If conventional medicine hadn't worked, a midwife could use spells to stop a mother haemorrhaging. This kind of practical work is known as low magic. Similarly, if you have a particular problem that you want to unfold, you might take a spirit walk. To do this, you need to find a stretch of land that you like to walk on. At the beginning of the walk you must knock on a stile or gate three times and ask the spirit of the roads to open. Coins or food are left as a thank you when you go in. You then walk along the pathway and keep thinking about your problem, all the time being observant of twig formations and any kind of wild animal interaction or event whilst you are walking along. You might find that branches form a pattern on the floor, like a rune. Walk along, hold an idea in your head and be open to your surroundings and an answer will be provided. It's as simple as that.

---

8. *Two children with an unusual green skin colour appeared in the village of Woolpit in the 12th century. The brother and sister were of normal appearance but spoke an unknown language, and would only eat raw broad beans. After the girl learned to speak English she said they had come from Saint Martin's Land, a subterranean world inhabited by green people.*

A month ago, when I was particularly concerned about something, a kestrel dropped down in front of me and did a little dance as I walked along the river. I did the same walk a number of times, and each time that bird did the exact same thing. Now, a kestrel has a superb view enabling it to drop down onto its prey. This kestrel, though, was actually dropping down onto me. There was no prey there at all. It told me that my perception wasn't right, that I needed to be more aggressive, to look at the situation from above and from outside the role of victim – swoop down on what you need or what you need to do in the situation. I did that, and as a consequence I left my job, which is what I wanted.

A simple barrier in a wooded glade on the Sweet Track walk

Earth and faery energies are not necessarily the same things. Earth energies can be like our energies – *chi* or *prana*. It's universal energy. Sometimes rock has a personality or spirit attached to it. Some places have a defined personality because there are spirits living there. So you might sense that that tree is a bit mischievous or is a healing tree; or think, I like that spot but not that one. That is mainly to do with spirit fauna and flora in the background as opposed to energy. Let's put it this way, if fairies were fish, the universal life force would be the sea that they swim in. The fish have different personalities and habits – one might swim at the top of the ocean, another in the middle and a third at the bottom. You never get two fish the same, just as you don't get two humans the same – but there are national characteristics.

There is a group of standing stones in Dorset called the Nine Stones. The site has railings around it and is overlooked by a big tree. I knew it had been worked by other witches before me as it felt calm, peaceful and connected – unlike the big stone circles which often feel touristy as people have connections with them intellectually not emotionally. With an emotional connection you pick

The Egg Stone set outside the Abbot's Kitchen at Glastonbury Abbey

Doorway to Lady's Chapel at Glastonbury Abbey ruins

up everything with your body as well as your mind. Earth magic, magic of this kind, is straightforward once you have the basic techniques. It is easy to do and to learn amazing things. Where the altar would have been was this spirit of a lady with long hair and a blue cloak. She started to talk to me. I knew she was the guardian of the circle. Whether it was the real guardian or an artificial one the witches had made, I'm not sure.

Conversely, most churches are built on Ley or Serpent lines, and have different chakra[9] points along the way. In a church or cathedral, the congregation and the bishops entered through different doors. While the congregation entered through a door to the south and sat down, the bishop or dignitary opened the great door and walked the whole length of the church to the altar, charging himself up energetically. You can retrace that path today and feel the energy. Although they didn't have words like Kundalini in the mediaeval period, people were dealing with the same things but under different names. This explains the plethora of serpents and dragons in churches.

9. *Chakras are the closest terminology we have in the modern world, but our ancestors would have understood the concept differently. We are talking about how the land or a building on it enhances the energy and can affect the energy body of the person experiencing it.*

Faery path between two trees

My axiom is that 'Magic is the art of relationships.' All herbs, plants, animals and stones have correspondences that relate to the greater energies of the planets which have influence on the earth plain. By putting some of these correspondences together it is like writing music. Like creating a flow of energy you want to manifest. For example, Beltane is about the marriage of male and female. The chalice represents the female and the *athame* (sword or knife) is male. I unite them in water, charge them up with magical energy and drink it as a wine. It is the same with the cauldron and staff. The remainder of the liquid is poured onto the land as a libation or a blessing. Another thing I do is to blend incense, perhaps with jasmine to represent the Goddess, and honeysuckle to represent the horned God. I blend these dried plants with Frankincense and Myrrh (also male and female) then add a dash of consecrated red wine and leave it overnight to absorb into the mixture. They are then ready to burn as an offering.

Beltane is a particularly powerful time to charm intimate relationships towards you. Essences can be used to attract the ideal partner.

Take an A4 piece of paper and draw a line from top to bottom. At the top of one side write 'you' and at the top of the other 'me'. For everything you desire in your partner put something the other side of the line to counterbalance it.

Once you have finished your list, soak your partner's half in the appropriate essence and then allow it to dry. Fold it up and seal it in an envelope. Place a green candle safely on top of the envelope which has been sprinkled with cinnamon, brown sugar and vanilla. Take greaseproof paper, put olive oil on it and then the cinnamon, brown sugar and vanilla. Take the green candle and roll it towards you so they stick to the outside of the candle. Do this 3 times. Roll, pick up, roll, pick up and roll again. You then place the candle on top of the letter in the south west corner of your working space, and in your own words call on the God and Goddess and the spirit Kadamel to witness and call forth your best partner.

You will begin to feel there is an essence in the room. If you gaze into the flame you will get a sense of your future partner's presence. You snuff out the flame when you have had your fill and say thank you to the God and Goddess and to the spirit of Kadamel for drawing your ideal partner to you. Ask Kadamel to return to her habitation in peace as she came in power. Sense that the room is back to normal. Do something completely mundane such as eating or watching TV. From this point on, you can simply light the candle for a few moments and talk to your partner until their arrival.

Be wary, though! There is a fall-out to this spell. You will get a rash of romantic dates. Old problems will appear with new faces. They will represent all the mistakes you have made in previous relationships, but they will give you the chance to end them differently. Only once this has all played out, will your new lover arrive.

Chapter 6
Litha – 21st / 22nd June

They've ploughed, they've sown, they've harrowed him in
Threw clods upon his head,
And these three men made a solemn vow
John Barleycorn was dead.

They've let him lie a very long time,
'til the rains from heaven did fall,
And little Sir John sprung up his head
and so amazed them all.

They've let him stand 'til Midsummer's Day
'til he looked both pale and wan,
And little Sir John's grown a long, long beard
and so become a man.

Old John Barleycorn, anonymous

Litha is the second great turning point of the solar year. A time of abundance when life rushes forth and the Earth is full and fertile and each person is required to surrender to nature's intelligent, intended plan.

Also known as the Summer solstice, Midsummer's eve, Midsummer's Day or St John's Day, Litha is the most powerful day of the year for the Sun God – when the sun is at the height of its power. The longest day is marked with carnival processions of light, candlelight and bonfires; circular processions and cartwheels of straw are kept in motion as the wheel of the year stops to start again.

Accompanying this celebration of bounty, the time of our dark inner world begins. The place of both light and dark as part of the whole is acknowledged.

LIVVY – Horse Whisperer

Livvy is the founder of **Paintedhorse CIC,** *an equine-facilitated learning business, which helps people gain clarity, perspective and the confidence to start living the life they truly want. Her twelve horses and ponies, stabled near Glastonbury in the UK, provide experiential learning along with their human facilitators.*

Livvy's work in the police force has given her a particular interest in women suffering from abuse, vulnerable people and prisoners.

Paintedhorse *works with a variety of groups within the community –* **Looked After Children, Help for Heroes** *and* **Key4Life** *which works with at risk young men from Somerset, Dorset and London within the prison system.*

Day One

We took four horses into Portland prison with the charity Key4Life, as part of a rehabilitation pre-release program for prisoners aged between eighteen and twenty-six. The idea is that the horses help the young men begin to recognise and deal with their emotions. There are thirty young men on the program split into two groups. One group does the Behaviour Change and Emotional Resilience work whilst the other works with the horses, and then they swap over. Interestingly, the group which works with the horses first seems to get more out of the second activity, since their minds have been opened to a different way of being.

The horses are all loose on the rugby pitch within the prison, which is surrounded by a high wall. When the first group comes out, I usually take them through an exercise to ground and centre them. It is a body scan basically, just so they are aware of where they are, what they are feeling if anything, and whereabouts in their body they're feeling it. We don't attach any meaning to it. It's the first sense of looking inwards for a lot of them. We ask them to close their eyes, which can be quite a big ask. When you're in a prison environment you don't generally close your eyes because you don't know what's behind you. The majority were happy to.

We were working with some of the trickiest prisoners in there. I personally don't want to know what they have done prior to their sentence. I don't want any preconceptions. I had a team of three girls for whom I was responsible. We had one facilitator per horse.

The first exercise is to meet the herd. It's about walking up to the horse slowly, and seeing what you notice. Is the horse moving away from you? Is it turning its head? What are its ears doing? Those little things you don't notice unless you look. All the signals the horse is giving you, saying *You're moving too fast! Go away!* or *You can come, it's okay.*

The horses were two geldings and two mares who all knew each other. One gelding lived with the two mares in one field, and the other gelding lived in a separate field. We had quite an interesting dynamic play out. One of the geldings was protecting his mares, whilst one of the mares wanted to be with the other gelding. It got quite animated at times. The young men were able to relate it to their own experience. One of them said, 'That's just like my girlfriend – *Come here! Now go away!*' They were noticing what was going on with the horses and relating it to their own lives.

We then split the groups into smaller groups so it was three or four young men with each facilitator. We approached the horses and all split up and circled round – unintentionally producing typical predator behaviour. The horses took off, and went for a little canter. So these really tough guys were hiding behind me because there was a horse galloping towards them. You forget how majestic and scary it is for someone who has no knowledge of horses to have half a ton of animal running towards you. You don't know that it won't run into you. They certainly didn't. Obviously, we do everything we can to keep them safe.

One of the geldings kept going to the far corner and the others followed. We retrieved him but he kept going back there. Speaking to the prison guards afterwards, they told me that that is the vulnerable point in the prison. If you were going to escape that's where you would go to because there's only a single wall to freedom. Everyone in the prison knows that. All the young men with their minds on an upcoming release date knew that. That's where their energy was. That's where the horses went to.

Then we moved onto another exercise in which we were trying to get them to work together. The horse is very much their partner. It's quite simple, it's leading. It's using their energy to get the horse moving. I explain that the head is the *stop zone*, the neck is the *friend zone* and behind the shoulder is the *go zone*. So if you want the horse to move, you direct your energy there. It's getting them used to using their energy and energetic fields. The horses had head collars on and the young men had ropes so they were able to lead them. They would work as a team of four, and they had a little obstacle course to navigate. So they had to think where they would stand at all times without blocking the horse.

Then we swapped the rope for a hula hoop, with two of them holding the hoop. There was no force on the horse at all. It was their energy communicating with the horse so they all moved together as one unit. If you try and drag a horse, it will resist and pull back. So the idea was that they were using their energy to get the horse to move, but some of that was travelling up the rope. It's about them all thinking forward and using their energy to get the horse to walk.

Day Two

On the second day they all got to ride. Again, we did a grounding exercise first, to get them to really breathe and centre. We had a mounting block so they weren't pulling the horses around as they were getting on. It was really quite ceremonial. They had to be in a really positive place to mount the horse. They had to ask the horse if it was okay to get on, and breathe in as they mounted.

They worked in teams, so somebody from the charity would be leading, as well as someone from their team, and they had two side-walkers to catch them if they slipped. Everything was done at walk and a little bit of trot. We took them through a series of exercises. So they were walking to get used to the feel of the horse beneath them, and then I got them to close their eyes and notice the sensations, and any changes. Then going down the long side of the prison I got them to put their arms out either side with their eyes closed and asked them if they could be anywhere in the world where they would be right now? That was very liberating for an awful lot of them – *I feel like I'm flying! I'm on a beach! I'm in Cuba...* It was bitterly cold, but the sun was out above the wall against a clear blue sky and they were riding with their eyes closed.

A couple more exercises – they had to stop the horse using only their breath. As they were breathing out they had to think 'Stop!' and lean back very slightly. Sometimes the horse would stop, sometimes it would slow down. It had to come from the rider, not the leaders. This was a huge revelation, that they could affect something else energetically without words. It brings that awareness of how as a person you affect other people simply by being you. If you're walking down the street and your energy's right out here because you're not looking very happy, it has an impact on those around you. It's just bringing that awareness back to yourself.

Once they'd all finished riding, I gave them strips of fabric on which to write their hopes and dreams for the future. Then they chose a horse and tied the fabric to the horse's mane and the horse took it outside for them. There was one young lad who, according to the prison and the charity, was the most difficult. A gang leader, really tricky and violent. Yet he did not want to tie his fabric in the horse's mane because he didn't want to hurt her. So he tied it to the reins instead and stroked her neck really gently.

The young men all have to apply to be on the program. There was 100 per cent attendance on both days, which is unheard of, apparently. This was the second program, and there was a lot of word of mouth. Also, the men are locked up 23 hours out of 24 some days, and it's something different.

Once the horses were outside, I took the fabrics out and tied them to one of the trees in the orchard. So their messages were there, and the wind took them. Although I didn't deliberately read them, some of them caught my eye: they want a job, they want to find love, they want success, they want to be happy. It's our basic human needs. It's what anybody wants. The press give this picture that they are bad people and need to be kept away; yet they are ordinary young men who've made bad choices and deserve a chance. The work they did with the horses, their engagement... They really want to change, they just need a helping hand.

Preparation

We sourced the horses from a local riding school. I picked four and did a trial run to see how they reacted together. But you don't know how they'll react in a prison in that kind of environment. They were alert and interested. The first day there were three chestnuts and one bay. On the second day, the bay went lame, so we had four chestnuts. We were able to differentiate between them because one had a flaxen head and tail, one was a tall ex-racehorse and so forth. They had to be of a certain size to carry the young men. At one point, one young man was standing in his stirrups overlooking the top of the wall.

The day before, I did some breathing exercises with my girls. We did a body scan to centre ourselves. I reminded them that during the day if at any time they felt it was going out of control, to imagine roots coming out of their feet and ground themselves. It's about being present and in the moment, and being grounded so that you can hold the space to allow the work to unfurl.

I wore similar clothing to them: jeans, boots, lots of layers, a jacket and a little hat to keep my ears warm. To get away from a uniform. The prison guards are in black and white. I wore a bright red jacket to stand out from everyone else, so people could see me if they needed to.

On Litha

At the Summer Solstice, I welcome in the sunrise and give thanks for all that has been. Generally I sit in meditative silence, call in my guides and thank them for their help and assistance over the year. After a short time, I begin to drum to raise some healing energy then send that energy into the world to be used where it is most needed to bring about positive change.

I mark the full moon and the new moon, as well as the dark moon (the day before the new moon) in ceremonies at Glastonbury. For me, the new moon signals new beginnings, a new start, what you might want to think about doing – things you want to bring into your life. It is also for expressing gratitude for what you have, acknowledgement. Drumming raises energy, as does singing and dancing. I light a fire and make my offerings.

Conversely, the full moon is about what you want to let go of. Intention is important. It can be as simple as going outside and acknowledging the moon. One doesn't have to be all singing and all dancing. You don't have to wear the dress. One can use an object as a tool – be they crystals or horses! If you don't have a crystal, you can pick up a stick and ascribe it with that meaning.

Horses are key to my changing my behaviour so that I was not re-enacting my trauma. Horses are masters of gestalt therapy. They make you live in the here and now and make you look at stuff you don't want to look at. They won't let you not look at it. They bring it up, sometimes by acting out your traumatic scenarios, and you work through it. They support you and then they let it go and you let it go, even working as a herd on occasion, sharing it out. The horses put themselves forward to help resolve different issues, for example anxiety, self-esteem, boundaries and bullying. I once saw a horse eating at a frantic pace in the company of a woman with an eating disorder. Horses are predisposed to then shake off their worries, such as after a predator has appeared and disappeared. We could learn from this.

Tied in its branches
are ribbons of dreams,
from men with dark futures, or so it seems.
The tree in the orchard
is no ordinary tree,
with roots firmly planted in Glastonbury.
With the mystery of Avalon
below and above,
the tree gives its dreamers unconditional love.
Wishes come true
and magic can happen
when we engage with our light and break our old patterns.
From a small seed
this tree grew stronger, grew wiser,
it knew the shit it went through was life's fertiliser.

Georgie McBurney

Chapter 7
Lughnasadh – 31st July / 1st August

The flute of interior time is played whether we hear it or not,
What we mean by "love" is its sound coming in.
When love hits the farthest edge of excess, it reaches a wisdom.
And the fragrance of that knowledge!
It penetrates our thick bodies,
It goes through walls —
Its network of notes has a structure as if a million suns were
arranged inside.
This tune has truth in it.
Where else have you heard a sound like this?

Kabir, Robert Bly Translation

Lughnasadh is a time of celebration, when we honour that which has helped us. Often a sacrifice is required to achieve something new.

Lughnasadh, or *loaf-mass*, is the feast which commemorates the funeral games of Lugh, the Celtic god of light. It is when the Sun God transfers his power into the grain and is sacrificed for the harvest in preparation for his return to the underworld. As the grain is gathered and the sun begins to wane, the earth gets ready to rest.

The first loaves baked from the harvest celebrate the abundance of Mother Earth. There is an emphasis on the cyclic rhythms of time and natural laws. As with the process of gestation and birth, at this time we understand nature, the life of all growing things and the ripening of things at the appropriate time.

CHLOË – Authentic Voice

Chloë is an international singer, innovatory educator, author and founder of The Naked Voice *(1990) which was awarded UK Charitable Foundation status in 2004. It is dedicated to the realization of compassionate communication in all realms of human life; as disseminated through the work of trained facilitators and dedicated learning communities called singing fields.*

Chloë has sung for H.H. Dalai Lama at The Good Heart conference *at London University and at* The Way of Peace, *a world conference held in Northern Ireland. She was music director and composer of* The Vagina Monologues *with acclaimed playwright Eve Ensler in Madison Square Gardens NYC.*

On the morning of September 11th 2001, Chloë was flying over New York in a United Airlines plane destined for San Francisco. This profound experience led to her performance in Transforming September IIth *at the Royal Opera House, London.*

In the last moments of my father's passing I was — quite literally — called to sing with him. Being a Christian priest, he had asked me to set the psalms, along with the Lord's Prayer, to music. I had never honoured his wish, and so now was my chance. Being a passionate choral singer in adolescence, I had loved singing a wide repertoire of Western sacred music, first in London choirs, and later as a university student in Cambridge. However, I fell in love with world music as an adult, especially classical Indian and Middle Eastern vocal sounds.

I realised how blessed I was to be with my father at this moment, and thought about all the times I had not been, travelling abroad. As I started to sing the Lord's Prayer, I noticed his breathing had changed. His lungs had begun to fill and an audible gurgle was rising from his throat. As I watched and listened to him now, I became fascinated by what he was going through as his physical body-mind prepared to let go.

As I started singing, 'Our Father who art in heaven, hallowed be Thy name,' I soon felt that I should simplify, focusing solely on the lines, 'Thy will be done, Thy kingdom come.' I had previously written a prayer set to a beautiful sanskrit melody, inspired by one of 20th century India's great female luminaries, Anandamayi Ma (Blissful Mother). I had once been lucky enough to sing this in a sacred Hindu temple in the presence of the *vedic* priests there. They had all magically appeared and sat down to meditate whilst I was singing. It was a glorious experience and a privilege to chant in the presence of these wise beings. A French *sannyasin* (renunciate nun) approached me immediately afterwards, and said, 'You are a devotee of Anandamayi Ma, aren't you?' I bowed. She had recognised the chant, as she had once heard Anandamayi Ma singing it. Her response to my rendition was that there was just one note I had got wrong! This was a poignant moment, and a reminder of the power of a melodic line to transmit a particular emotional tone, or spiritual message. One altered musical note could shift the essential meaning and *bhav* (emotion) of the whole song or chant.

This call to precision reminded me of a story about a monk in the *Tibetan Book of Living and Dying*. The monk has just died when his master comes in and exclaims, 'No, no you don't die like that. Come back!' On hearing his teacher, the monk comes back to life again. His master then conducts him through the correct way to release his body-mind and to die according to the precise Tibetan rituals. This story made a profound impression on me, demonstrating the significance of transparency and skillfulness when undertaking a rite of passage, or a transformative shift from one cycle of life to another. In this case, it was the journey from physical death into a new life beyond.

So I was singing 'Thy will be done' with my father as he moved around in his bed whilst courageously trying to sing with me. His voice sounded primal. Yet this was his prayer now. As a protestant priest, he had been an obedient servant of God, and an inspiring preacher, always dedicated to his life-long vocation. Now he was on the threshold of this life, and it was here that he revealed how his life on Earth was fulfilled. I felt it strongly. As I continued singing, 'Thy will be done,' he tried to join me. It was as if he was throwing off outworn clothes, the old layers of himself. I have an image of him butterflying backwards, falling back into an ocean of being. When I reached the words 'for Thine is the kingdom' he seemed to be in a kind of mystical ecstasia, pouring his whole self, vulnerability, everything, into the song. He then reached the point where he had exhausted expressing himself. As this spontaneous ceremony came to an end he became very quiet. The atmosphere became very quiet. His eyes were open, his face was calm, and by this point the rest of the family had assembled around his bed.

As we all watched him in silent awe, I suddenly felt as if I was accompanying him beyond this world. It was like a birthing process in reverse. He began to relax and his breath became simple and clear. I don't know how that happened. The Cheyne-Stokes respiration was replaced by a very gentle breathing. He was breathing in, and then out. We were all breathing with him: Is this the last breath? No, it's not, there is another one... Then he brought my brother's forehead very close to his own. I watched their two strong profiles, foreheads locked together, in an extraordinary moment between father and son. They looked each other in the eye. It was intense, like a transmission. Then my brother drew back and my father breathed again, slowly in and out. Eyes wide open, he took three more breaths. At the last breath he breathed in, and finally looked out. His gaze was directed far into the cosmos. Then he closed his mouth, breathed his last and left. It was a seamless and simple transition, followed by the deepest peace which filled the whole room.

The moment was so potent that I actually found myself travelling out with him. I've never experienced that before. It was as if I left this world with him, passed through an invisible passage and joined his new journey beyond this world. Everything became very abstract. It was impersonal and ethereal. For about two weeks I felt as if I were floating above the floor. I had the sense that I had gone somewhere before the world was made, beyond our story of father and daughter in this lifetime. It was an immense privilege.

Two weeks after the funeral, I was working in New York and a friend there encouraged me to visit a well-known psychic. She is a remarkable human being. As I entered her eccentric apartment she was sitting on a throne. She looked at me and said, 'Someone has just died, haven't they? Was it your father?' Then a compelling conversation unfolded about my relationship with my dad: his ambivalence and disillusionment with the constraints of the patriarchal church and his acknowledgement of my own mystical relationship with Christ consciousness, as influenced by other religious and wisdom traditions. I shared how he had once looked at me with a twinkle in his eye, saying, 'When I die I will see Christ, and when you die, you will see your teacher, Anandamayi Ma the Great Mother.' My conversation with the New York psychic brought me back to earth. I put my feet back on the ground. I turned around and was able to consciously face my own life once more.

Reflecting on an earlier experience of my father's vocation, I remember the day in 1964 when Archbishop Michael Ramsey consecrated my father as a suffragan (assistant) London bishop, in St Paul's Cathedral. We all accompanied my father who was staying at Lambeth palace, the home of Archbishop Ramsey. I was eleven. I remember Michael Ramsay reading a passage from St John's gospel in which Christ is anticipating his own death and resurrection in the Garden of Gethsemane. It was three days before his crucifixion and entombment. Christ finally transmits His final message to His disciples who have fallen asleep in the Garden. Christ knows He will leave this world soon. The final surrender. Thy will be done.

Before my father parted from this world, he left me with an essential message: 'Go to the places where I couldn't go.' This left a profound impression, especially as my father had played such a huge role in the cause of women priests. His respect for my own vocation to bring the potent presence of the sacred feminine into the world was very clear.

I now have to surrender to a much deeper understanding of the impact of the transforming power of spirit through sound – individually and collectively – as a *gnostic* wisdom, a direct experience of Love's unconditional presence, inspired by non-dual and compassionate communication, in the world.[10] The human voice is the sacred bridge between our personal soul and universal spirit. The more I learn to embody my authentic voice, the more deeply I can surrender into the fierce and gentle compassion of Love's infinite will. To sing 'Thy Will Be Done' is to invoke and to integrate my highest aspirations with my grounded purpose on Earth. My spiritual teacher Anandamayi would exclaim: 'Destroy the veil that hides your own Self. Death itself must die. Discover the illusion of death before you drop the body. Realise your human spirit as the divine radiance and luminosity of a thousand

10. *'Non-dual' communication derives from advaita in Indian spiritual philosophy, meaning non-separateness, oneness.*

suns. Let go, now! Release the endless attempts we make every day to separate ourselves from our deep Self, from each other, from this present moment… and from this one… and from this.'

The surrender that my father taught me in the last sacred moment of his physical life was a gift of fierce compassion, through the transmission of love's infinite presence.

When I first came back from India in 1990 following a transformative no-mind experience, the words of my non-dual teacher Poonjaji (Papaji) rang in my head: 'When you return to the UK, just keep quiet.' Sitting in blissful silence for hours was my greatest joy in those early days. Silence brought me closest to the heartbeat of existence. Silence, breath and deep listening. Gradually, as my ordinary self returned, singing became the alchemical bridge between my personal and transpersonal life. And so, I finally coined the phrase 'naked voice' — a voice whose wisdom is older and deeper than the polarity of all conflict.

It soon became clear to me that singing and expressing myself directly and authentically from my soul (as opposed to performative singing) was an essential untapped resource that could help me to remember my sovereign nature, and to reconnect with my divine origin. In the words of the poet David Whyte:

> To be human
> is to become visible,
> while carrying
> what is hidden
> as a gift to others.
>
> To remember
> the other world
> *in* this world
> is to live in your
> true inheritance.

Singing from the heart effortlessly and spontaneously became my practice. In 1990, I knew that I had to share this spontaneous prayerful singing, as an expression of my gratitude for the extraordinary transformation that had occurred in my life. So without further thought I found myself walking into a recording studio. As we recorded the sound falling out of my mouth, I was genuinely aware that it was coming from a source deeper than my own personal will. And I knew that it served a purpose beyond anything that my conceptual mind could fathom at that time.

Even though I was obviously responsible for expressing this new music of my spirit, a deeper channel of sound awareness had opened up inside me that was entirely new. It carried an infinite spaciousness of its own that 'Chloë' simply had to listen to, follow and obey. I had happened upon the source of Life itself, and 'Chloë' was simply a conduit or a channel for the sound. I had no knowledge that this would be my life's work, beyond the fact that sharing sound and sharing gratitude for the grace of this new Life itself were the only things that made sense to me. Singing, music and especially vocal sound had been my life's passion. Were I a gardener, say, I would probably have transmitted it through the creation of gardens; or as a painter, through artwork.

A certain 'sacrifice' accompanied this new understanding. In sloughing off my old personality, I found I had to surrender my attachment to my old self for the resonance of the naked sound to be heard. To surrender to the inevitable outpouring and offering up of gratitude. The sacrifice is the gift offering, returning that which is 'sacred' back into life. Sacrificing your old self, you make a sacred offering of your new self into the world, whilst simultaneously giving up all identity with being 'the doer.' This brings us back to 'Thy will be done.' Embodying what that truly means is a lifetime's exploration, and this was my father's last precious gift to me.

In the years that followed I have enjoyed placing myself in the presence of authentic, original, indigenous peoples who live very close to the land and honour their life in accordance with Mother Nature and the ebb and flow of the seasons as a gift to the world. The process of living in the now, or consciously letting go of what is past, is essential. That is why self-inquiry is an essential part of the Naked Voice understanding. Ask yourself questions, such as: Who is singing? Who is breathing? What quality of silence does my voice leave behind? Who is making this journey? Who is propelling my every step, my thoughts?

Other questions arise. Does our perception of what we see externally trigger what moves internally? Is our attention governed more from the outside—in or the inside-out?

When Christ was in the Garden of Gethsemane, for example, His external reality was the Pharisees, the scribes and Judas — the whole self-pleasing, ego-driven world — of diverse peoples of conflicting beliefs. What was actually faced there by Him at that moment was the collective unconscious ego distracted by fear, separateness, and death. Where did the strength come from to navigate and transcend such darkness, confusion and misunderstanding? How was Christ able to be so embodied and internally free that He could transcend the nightmare of orthodoxy and the status quo? I often say to people, when your ego shows up don't resist it or push it away. See it as a little bird eating out of your hand. Let it know that it has a new job — no longer one of separating and casting negative judgement, rather to wonder at the world; to be curious, fascinated, genuinely interested and unafraid.

Christ in the Garden was faced with the ultimate ego confrontation, that of physical death itself. How did He respond? There was a moment of hesitation... then He went through. Was it cosmic intervention?

There was this incredible moment of grace in which He realized that He had to die to demonstrate that death itself must die; death, that is an illusion of the ego mind. And that's what I saw in my father in the moment that his breath stopped. And that is what I am learning to embody and embrace now.

There is no death. It both is and it isn't true. The body does die. There is no way that our ordinary mind can comprehend that passing. An awareness deeper than the limitations of the conceptual mind has to be embodied before this shift in understanding can occur. Mystics, including Pierre Teillhard de Chardin, call it union with the Beloved, unification with the universal awakening to the planetary mind. Our relationship with our conceptual mind has to dissolve and transform into what Goethe called a 'higher lovemaking.'

Papaji told me this lovely story about how he was once sitting with the meditation teacher Krishnamurti having a public spiritual dialogue.

'Krishna Murti told me that he removes the furniture from the mind.' Then an incredible smile came over Papaji's face as he stared directly at me and said, 'I remove the mind altogether !' The practice of your naked voice is a process of grace and gradual revelation. By grace, not human effort, it too can remove your conceptual mind altogether. And that is a journey 'beyond right and wrong doing'.

I'll meet you there.

Chapter 8
Mabon – 22nd / 23rd September

O go you onward; where you are
  Shall honour and laughter be,
Past purpled forest and pearled foam,
  God's winged pavilion free to roam,
Your face, that is a wandering home,
  A flying home for me.

Ride through the silent earthquake lands,
  Wide as a waste is wide,
Across these days like deserts, when
  Pride and a little scratching pen
Have dried and split the hearts of men,
  Heart of the heroes, ride.

Up through an empty house of stars,
  Being what heart you are,
Up the inhuman steeps of space
  As on a staircase go in grace,
Carrying the firelight on your face
  Beyond the loneliest star.

Take these; in memory of the hour
  We strayed a space from home
And saw the smoke-hued hamlets, quaint
  With Westland king and Westland saint,
And watched the western glory faint
  Along the road to Frome.

from **The Ballad of the White Horse, G.K. Chesterton**

Mabon is a time to reap what you have sown and give thanks for the harvest and bounty the Earth provides. A time to finish old projects and thank those who have helped us – to celebrate and plan for the future.

The Autumn Equinox or Mabon is a time of equal day and night. The old Sun God journeys into the winter lands and returns to the Goddess. His passing is inevitable and should not be mourned.

Mabon is a time of celebration and balance. A time to harness our more instinctual nature, accept the consequences of our actions and own the vital forces within. To realise the potential integration of opposites within our personality, and experience being whole. This permanent end to a cycle of life needs to be acknowledged before new opportunities might arise.

FFYONA – Hunter Gatherer

Ffyona has spent many years exploring the world on foot and learning from Australian Aborigines, African Bushmen, Pygmies and North American Indians.

In 1997 she returned home to learn the wild food of her native land.
Ffyona leads wild food walks teaching people about our edible and poisonous native plants and the hunter-gatherer life we once loved.

When I go out to gather wild food or explore, I look at everything with a sense of joy and love. There's a smell that goes with every emotion, a bi-product. A blackberry loves being a blackberry. A skylark loves being a skylark. An oak tree loves being an oak tree. They are producing love. So I realise that what the world produces is love. Don't all the religions say that it is love that creates the universe?

Wild things are perfect within their selves. They are not judging, criticizing or doubting themselves. When I watch people gather pig nuts I can feel and hear the absorption. Whether they've come from London or Brighton or are worried about their careers, there's a sound that happens, when people start to make this little sound instead of talking. It sounds like birds. The general tones of their voices start lifting. It is humankind's natural sound. Almost a joyful trilling, with exclamations as well. The language that any human on Earth can understand is those sounds… That's the human song.

We take plants for granted. Because we can pick them, the Western mind thinks they must be stupid. One day, I was hammering through the undergrowth and cut to pieces in the filthiest, muddiest, marshiest place you could find. 'Why are you going through all this just to gather mushrooms,' I asked myself. 'How is the mycelium getting me to do this?' Then I became conscious of the smell of the mushrooms. Just loving that smell is my carrot, my promised reward. Eating the mushroom is so uplifting. Not in any psychological or psychedelically changing way but in a life-is-good way. We don't really have phrases like that for good any more – for happiness. It's an earthly joyfulness, a deep-down feeling rather than an up-top feeling. This is a rightness, a reward as deep as you can get.

It's desire that motivates us, isn't it? The connection or cord is through smell. It's not conscious to begin with. Although you're unaware of it, you are walking towards the aroma. You think, 'I know it will be around that corner.' And there it is.

The first thing we encounter is smell. Do you remember as a child just how powerful your olfactory senses were? I went to fifteen different schools and smell was the first thing which would tell me I was in a school. Then I would just get choked up and start to get a really tinny taste. The other kids were always staring at me because I was the new girl. Each school smelt different. There was a powerfulness of smell back then. Now I don't notice it much at all. I'm not walking into a bank of smells. If we were hunter gatherers we would still have that. If we could have the sense of smell we enjoyed as children, we would each be able to walk into a room and know who was frightened. You would know so many things just by the smell of them. When Africans used to get frightened of me, the fear would turn to anger and they would suddenly stink. I knew, 'My God, I am in trouble!' when I smelt that. An acrid smell. It's very strong. You know that you have found something when you smell that smell.

The olfactory system is very well-developed and I'm sure that 90% of it occurs unconsciously. Around Mahon in these horrendous marshes, going on a trail to find something that is only four inches across, I was imperceptibly led by smell. The moment of seeing a mushroom there is a shot of dopamine. It's such a greeting. Hello! It's a very human encounter with an old friend. I have looked for wild food with Pygmies, Bushmen and Aborigines, but I first learned with Ray Mears when we were in our early twenties before he decided to go onto bush-craft and make that his career. In fact, he was the first one to take me out mushrooming. It was a lot about smell. Not that either of us was very aware of it. One of the people he learned from was a mushroom expert who was always smelling mushrooms and getting so much joy from it. This man always had a mushroom under his nose.

I notice when I am being repelled by a plant. At the end of garlic's life when it doesn't want us to pick it, it has this bad smell. It doesn't necessarily look like it has gone off but there's no mistaking the smell. It makes me nauseous. When we get to autumn and you start sniffing oak leaves, you will notice some of them smell sweet like candy-floss. It's a hormone that oak leaves produce that helps everyone prepare for the winter. It makes you start gathering in and wanting to sleep as well. Some of the smaller animals drag oak leaves into their burrows and sleep on them so they have sweet dreams.

When I first encountered Herb Bennett, it was just this stalky plant with a pretty yellow flower on. It kept banging against my leg wherever I went, trying to get my attention. So, I said, 'Okay, I will find out who you are.' As well as being Herb Bennett it was also known as Saint Benedict's Herb. For a plant to be both given the name 'herb' and the name of a saint is a very special thing. Nobody really knows about the important properties of this plant. We know it can protect you from snake bites, but other things must have been forgotten as well. I went back to it and asked, 'Who are you?' I was being drawn in. Nothing else was in my vision but this plant. I looked at it and it was getting bigger and bigger in my eyes. I could actually see tiny little details in its flowers. If you look really intensely at something it grows. I've seen this with snails. I look into a snail's eye and suddenly the snail has grown so big that I can actually see the expression in its eye. I feel like I am going somewhere when I am doing that. Entering an intense dialogue.

In the early autumn, at East Prawle on the Devonshire coast, I time my group wild-food walks so the tide is fully out and seaweed is exposed to my scissors and open-weave basket. I work in silence, then sit on a rock close to the incoming waves. I point out the smooth reddish-purple Carrageen Moss, the Dulse which tastes like smoky bacon and the Kelp found near the lower shore with its broad, flat lengths that can be used like lasagna sheets. During the walk I show each group the natural energy enhancers, a suntan cream, a skin repairer and a seaweed full of iodine. I speak of laver seaweed made into a paste called Laverbread used by Welsh miners to sustain them during long working shifts, and of natural contraception.

The plants dictate their own needs – carrots and plums like to seed close together. Nature's design and the plants' encouragement help them to be 'dug up' or 'weeded out' by human hunter gatherers who find a succulent patch hard to resist. This is essential for the survival of the rest. I find loose badger poo near the plum trees – re-depositing the seed close by, and in line with the trees' wishes to grow close together. In the desert, the Acadia tree does not like close neighbours, so its edible parts encourage constipation.

Each plant emits a scent. When I'm running at night I smell the plants really strongly. I can't see them but I know who is in there. I first noticed this in the winter. It was a warm day, just after the full moon at the solstice. That was the first night I had smelt the plants all winter. Because they had been warmed they started to grow. Each smell was a song: 'I am Holly and I am alive' or 'I am Hawthorn and I am alive.' That's what it sounded like. Like a parfumier smelling different notes. When I listen to the birds singing their dawn chorus it makes me think of the plants who sing their evening chorus. Have you noticed that things smell more in the evening and at dawn and then lose their smell during the day? In the evening it's easy for smells to be transported. I drink it in like a cool elixir.

Plants draw me in with their smell, then I see them and feel the same delight as when I see a friend. It's uncomplicated and I don't feel nervous. They give me unconditional love. I look at them and can see the whole being that they are. As with Jack by the Hedge, there is always a leaf that's superfluous. A good leaf at the back that's not really getting any sun which I can take and the plant has been relieved of it. I do it because that is what feels natural. I'm pruning the plant, but because I'm going to eat it, rather than put it on the compost heap. I know when I look at it where it is too bushy. Jack by the Hedge has this perfect posy on the top which is just so pickable. Pick that one and two more grow back. When the seed heads come it is no longer so pickable and two won't grow back if you pick one. It has a different smell which we pick up subliminally.

The goal of freedom is programmed in us, a part of us. Ironically, it is when a tree manipulates us that we feel most free. Take mycelium, the biggest organism on earth. Nothing would happen without it. It breaks everything down. We do a job for it by picking the mushrooms. Yet plants reward us tenfold because we pick ten of their nuts and inadvertently drop only one. When people manipulate us, we are robbed of both soul and spirit. The plants satisfy us. Wild food satisfies us. It's a fair exchange.

My Wheel of the Year

Jenny, author

I began to *wake up* in the late autumn of 2015. This was assisted by the natural world and familiar places from my childhood and youth which called to me gently. As you have seen, a series of bards, hags, shrews, soothsayers, sorcerers, shamans and witches — call them what you will — came to my aid. Practitioners revered for their wisdom, powerful and respected seers, herbalists and healers enchanted me with their gentle work, probing my subconscious over the long months. As we worked together, I became immersed in the landscape, vibrational medicine and magic — along with the cycles and rhythms of nature and the movements of the moon, sun and planets. They provided a frame of reference. A new way of seeing and understanding life and the natural powers that govern us.

My teachers had come to know themselves and become 'at one' with nature through profound immersive experiences. Journey, ritual or meaningful connections enabled them to embody something else's nature which consequently demanded radical change of them. They turned towards energies for guidance — be it a Yew tree, a place (such as Wayland's Smithy) or an animal — which then turned towards them. The concept of calling into one's self is a standard part of magical practice. It is a possession of sorts, and if done properly one can remain under the control or direction of the energies one summons. Put simply, these people called on the characteristics they wanted to invoke.

Isla, queen of yew, tasted death by eating red berries at Samhain when the veil between the worlds is thinnest.

Tim, rune master, conducted deep shadow-work and brought the end of the ice and darkness by journeying into the spirit world. Freyr's golden bristled boar brought a time of new beginnings.

Forest, land spirit, walked every inch of her homeland to learn the dance of relationship and then entered the underworld of the druid king to review her dark and deeply-damaged side.

Eliana picked up and transmitted information through her hands. Her womb-work with disempowered women helped them mend their cracked and leaking cauldrons and reclaim their power tools.

David, hedge-rider, moved between worlds to merge with the land and trees and gather information. Spell work and low magic helped him to self-heal and change the mundane landscape.

Livvy, horse-whisperer, used animals to help prisoners get in touch with their senses and what was really going on in their world in order to give them another chance at a fulfilled life.

Chloë witnessed the ultimate sacrifice required both at the end of life and if one is to lose ego-consciousness during life, travelling with her father into the other world.

Ffyona, hunter-gatherer, returned to our ancient ways of living and connection in order to experience heart-based living and the felt sense.

These practitioners were a mirror to me during the year. This is why they were drawn to me in the first place. Each taught me a way of expressing my true self. Equally, the sky, land and creatures were my teachers. By seeing the land as a reflection of my own personal drama, it was possible to see my own predicaments embodied in my surroundings. Using the integral power and intelligence of animals and plants it is possible to reach a deeper connection with who you are and where you are from. The practitioners in this book take a holistic approach to healing beyond merely treating presenting ailments. Rather, they help to heal spiritual discomfort. To address people's spirits and souls.

In terms of my own understanding of the wheel of the year, it turned out that my lessons did not fall into a consecutive ordered pattern. Rather, by studying and living through the eight festivals, I came to realise new things about my life, and perhaps my own regeneration. However, it was my final interview, with a Dharma teacher, that drew the experiences together for me.

Mark, Dharma teacher

Irritated by the throat-clearing of a fellow monk which was interrupting his meditation, Mark found that by attributing the sound to someone close to his heart, he could turn it into something positive. This led him to believe that the universe was actually his to bend to his perception.

> The world impacts on me but also I impact the world. What's going on inside me, the qualities I have in my heart, the views I have in my mind, the assumptions I make and how I'm relating to the world on a perceptual level impacts on what I perceive. The totality of my world is my perception.

Similarly, he was able to put aside his own discomfort and dissatisfaction, and see events as beneficial to others as a whole. Just as he had asked,

> Could I go one step further and see this neutral sound as beautiful? Imagine the sound is like God kissing me? Like a divine embrace?

and almost began to long for that sound, he realised that this was all to do with *emptiness*.

If I decide to change what is in my heart and mind and it changes my experience of things for the better it seems like a good journey to go on. Rather than just trying to change things outside, I can cultivate various qualities in my heart. I can choose to look at the world in certain ways conceptually and a different reality appears for me.

So our way of looking at the world, changes the world.

In my own practice it is certainly not all day, every day that I practice *emptiness*. I might sink into some petty thought or wonder what is going to happen. Maybe a minute or an hour later I recognise I am creating something that need not be. Then, if I allow my heart to shift a bit I can create a totally different world. So I keep coming back to this idea that I am actively participating and creating in every moment.

Mark's description of how his world can change when viewed through different lenses prompted me to revisit my own myths. Many of these stories had now been outgrown and the way was clear for a different reality. One that like Mark's world relied on personal images, trust in my own experience and intuition, and was based on an authority within.

My wheel of the year started with the prophetic words of a Tarot reading.

This is a heck of an emotional journey. A lot of shadow-work needs to be done. People pull everything you have created apart but you have the power to shield yourself and protect others with your voice. The Tower card tells me things will be unsettled and some relationships choppy. You have a good idea where you want to go now and should trust your gut instinct. This ace signals a new job and different sources of income. There will be more study — an apprenticeship of sorts — with one person teaching you how to do something. The three of swords is the card of truth. A surprise. It usually turns up when we have been lying to ourselves or someone else is withholding information. The two of cups indicates strong friendships and people you love and trust. You will find solutions when you rest and take care of yourself. Be gentle with yourself. An amazing opportunity will come out of thin air.

Everything did change. Old wounds were revisited through carefully-orchestrated, practitioner-supported healings, journeys and voice work. On my quest for knowledge I found answers to hidden problems, and sudden changes and closures occurred. It was not easy. My career of thirty-five years came to an end and I struggled to find an authentic voice. A myriad of courses — involving earth-work, sound and trauma — kept me busy for a while. They gave me basic skills in dowsing, tuning-fork healing and the medicine wheel, along with how to deal with trauma re-enactments through healings and storytelling.

In 2017, a hunter-gatherer migration changed my perspective on life. My interest in horse whispering and equine-facilitated learning returned. Old teachers and friends got back in contact after a number of fallow years. In the summer, a kinesiologist corrected the balance of my neurotransmitters. An old chemical residue was affecting their performance. Most of all, an apprenticeship in rune divination, magic and healing helped me move to another stage, evolving out of the will (me) and into the heart (others). Use of shamanic journeying, drum-beats and rattles, chanting, ceremony, ritual, poetry and myth are all central to my practice.

Soon, I will have to immerse myself in other work, but first I will rest. In the meantime, I spend many happy hours walking the land, learning about trees and plants and visiting sacred sites. There is a growing harmony between my internal and external worlds. An unfamiliar joy or freedom has quietly entered my life.

A note on Trauma

(relating to Tim journeying to the subconscious realms to locate and remove trauma, Forest contacting and releasing 'monstrous' energies, Eliana working with traumatised women, Livvy working with prisoners who often have traumatic backgrounds and difficult family lives and Chloë assisting people to re-find their authentic voice following trauma, with speaking or singing.)

When we experience a life-threatening event, the 'fight or flight' and 'freeze or flood' response can become automatic. We resemble a trapped animal whose body gives in when it feels death is inevitable. Problems occur when, unlike an animal, we cannot shake off the trauma after the threat of death departs. An echo of the original trauma splits off and becomes trapped in the body's matrix, so although life continues we carry an emotional disturbance. This can be true even if our trauma experience is not life-threatening. If a teacher or person in authority criticizes us, causing us embarrassment and shame, or if we fall badly or have an accident resulting in pain and injury or are subject to abusive or violent behaviours — we may experience soul loss or a trauma that endures.

Research on trauma indicates that it affects the messages sent to our parasympathetic, sympathetic and social nervous system — which affects hormonal output — and can eventually result in lockdown. Physically, we may have problems breathing and communicating and may experience flashbacks. Similarly, our speech betrays our trauma: our tone of voice, our timing, Freudian slips and even our accompanying facial expressions. Other symptoms include a restricted ability to feel, handle change or move on from an unproductive situation. Being stuck in the arousal cycle[11] is common as is having unmet needs whilst continually meeting the needs of others.

Trauma reactions can result in constriction, dissociation and helplessness. Constriction is a numbing response in which self-control and life restrictions are used to manage fear. It is associated with obsessive compulsive disorder and agoraphobia. Dissociation is when people feel disconnected from the world around them or themselves. It helps to distance the experience from the individual. An individual might experience a distortion of time, space or identity. Conditions such as schizophrenia, bipolarity, personality disorders and post-traumatic-stress can result. Helplessness might include people who are unable to control their current environment, take action or make decisions (a learned helplessness). This is associated with avoidant behaviours such as self-medication (often including alcohol abuse) and compulsive behaviours

11. *Challenges or threats cause 'arousal'. When they are faced, our arousal peaks, reducing again afterwards leaving us relaxed.*

(such as overeating), impulsive, often high-risk, behaviours and/or self-injurious behaviours. In addition, it might include aggressive behaviours or subconscious re-enactments of aspects of the trauma.

Some trauma survivors relive, re-enact and recreate a past trauma in the present, unwittingly mimicking previous events. So the original drama is acted out in intimate relationships, work situations or repetitive accidents. The trauma survivor puts themselves in situations reminiscent of the original trauma in order to find new solutions.

Over time, symptoms can often translate into illness or disability whether it manifests as a broken ankle, bad back, depression, cancer or mental health issues. The variations are endless.

The focus of shamanic soul retrieval work is trauma release. Following a trauma, a pattern of tension is locked into the body whilst the kidneys hold the vibration of shock and fear. Stuck life-force sits like an electrical charge inside the memory. Once released, it allows us to assimilate and digest the experience.

Trauma survivors need to learn tools to deactivate the nervous system. The details of the trauma are not important in this process. What is critical is to not become invested in a literal truth – reliving the actual trauma experience. Our 'gestalts of experience' are categorised by the levels of activation at which they occur; we store and resolve our less-traumatic experiences first. If we desire to recover, and dissolve our feelings of shame, blame and need for revenge, we must be willing to let go and change our understanding of who we really are first. It is unlikely to happen all at once.

A note on Sound Healing

(relating to Isla connecting to the Yew tree with her drum, Tim using the harp and drum for healing journeys, Eliana's storytelling, Forest walking the land as a tympanic synaesthete, David's use of vibration and play in magic and Chloë's singing and chanting.)

All matter is vibrating. As such, the vibration of language, different symbols and the senses we use – sound, sight, feeling, smell, taste – can become tools for healing and magic. We can call things in, send things away and invoke prayer through vibration. If we surrender to a higher power, we can even ride or fly (with a spirit guide or animal helper) with the rhythm. Sound healing uses medicine objects such as tuning forks, Tibetan singing bowls, crystal bowls, didgeridoos, percussion instruments such as drums and rattles as well as chanting, sounding and singing as forms of therapy. These transmute and carry energy through sound vibration. The sound pulses dissolve areas of congestion allowing electricity, blood and lymph to flow more freely in the body. Certain tones or sounds promote healing and even allow DNA strands to repair themselves.

The Om tuning fork is said to be the sound of creation – the heartbeat of the Earth or a mother's love. It balances the right and left hemispheres of the brain and quietens the ego, aiding relaxation and sleep. The Schumann resonance – 7.83 Hz – is a universal electromagnetic wavelength said to be the frequency emanating from the hands of healers. This frequency gives us a sense of connection and Oneness. Audio tones and vibrational frequencies repair damaged body tissue and cells to cure arthritis, tumours, depression and stress. Sound can be used to deconstruct the concepts around our repressed emotions and return the previously-wasted energy to the system as a whole. Congestion in a person's energy field is reflected in their body, life situation or home environment. When areas previously associated with emotional clutter are cleared, chaos in the outer environment usually disappears as well.

Eileen McKusick, author of *Tuning the Human Biofield*, describes 'hearing the stories' in the dissonance of the overtones as tuning forks pass over the body. She listens to the quality of sound – volume, pitch and timbre (pain has a loud, sharp tone or one of static and noise). Then, like using a magnet to move iron fillings across a surface, she locates pockets, walls and fields of emotive energy and *combs* it from the periphery of the body to the vertical midline. The surface of our Earth has a negative polarity whilst our bodies have a positive polarity, McKusick maintains. As our shoes act as insulators for energy exchange it is good to walk barefoot – to act like a lightning rod and give your energy the chance to ground, rather than becoming stuck in your body.

The most commonly-accepted physical ailments, psychological disturbances, musical notes and Tao sounds associated with major organs in the body

Organ	Physical ailment	Psychological disturbance	Musical note	Tao sound
Lungs	Asthma, colds	Depression	G	Sssss
Kidney	Fatigue, dizziness	Fear	D	Woooh
Liver	Digestive problems	Anger	F#	Shhhh
Heart	Sore throat, coldsores	Impatience	B	Haaaw
Spleen, stomach & pancreas	Nausea, indigestion	Worry	A#, A, C#	Whoooo

Healing with the voice is an ancient technique. Chloë Goodchild states in *The Naked Voice* that the seven 'sounds of love' are gateways which provide a singing map inspired by the seven bodily energy centres. For her, specific ancient toning sounds interact with each of the chakras - SA (root), RE (pelvis), GA (solar plexus), MA (heart), PA (throat), DHA (third eye) and NI (back of head). Vocal exercises using these sounds, can be used to harmonise mind, body and soul. James D'Angelo, author of *The Healing Power of the Human Voice*, states:

> If the voice is a natural healing instrument, then the overtones are its aura, its bio-energetic field. It follows that the conscious production of overtones — that is, to make individual harmonics audible and hence to intensify them — increases the therapeutic capacity of the voice in certain respects.

The most commonly-accepted physical aspects, psychological disturbances and musical notes associated with chakras

Chakra	Physical Aspect	Psychological Disturbances	Musical Note
Root	Spinal column, kidneys	Insecurity	F
Sacral	Reproductive system	Powerlessness	G
Solar Plexus	Stomach, liver, gall bladder, nervous system	Fear	A
Heart	Heart, blood, circulatory system	Depression	C
Throat	Bronchial tubes, vocal cords, lungs	Lack of expression	D
Brow	Lower brain, left eye	Distorted thinking	Upper F
Crown	Upper brain, right eye	Loss of sense of self	Upper G

A note on Magic (based on David's interview)

(relating to Isla's connection to the trees, Tim's healing work, Forest's weather work, Eliana's womb-work and power tools, David's work in general, the use of horses as a form of Gestalt Therapy in Livvy's work, Chloë's seven sounds of love and Ffyona's work with plants.)

The universe works on resonance and everything has its own vibration. Every fraction of hair, nail clipping or piece of clothing represents the whole. This is how nine-tenths of magic is done. To work magic on someone without a correspondence is like guess-work. Saliva or ash can be used for a love potion or perhaps to influence someone's finances or encourage a reversal of fortunes. Sage and Oak are Jupitarian, and so linked to expansion and duality and banishing. Nettles are ruled by Mars, so linked with action and defence, taking away rubbish and dealing with negativity. Myrrh is linked to Saturn and restriction (useful if you have a boil and want to reduce it). Crystals and animals also have correspondences. You might encounter them in the field or in dreams. Over the centuries, the Aboriginals in Australia, the people of Africa and those in the Caribbean have all intuitively picked up the same message from each plant.

If you know how something interrelates with something else, you can work with it. If you can pick up a stone and know that it is ruled by Saturn, then you can work the spirit in that stone to bind somebody or something. The concept wouldn't be too far over the head of a child. In fact, the childlike mind – the sense of play, not over-thinking it – is part of the formula. A person is a creation of many different factors, inherited, environmental and cultural, and a magician going into a temple, glade or woodland can turn all of that off. The root of being successful is the ability to step out of your constructs. Any practice, such as casting a circle, will help you to do that.

Witchcraft in its purest form concerns magical power rather than religion although witches do work with Gods, Goddesses, Spirits and Saints, to affect the physical plain. That is why 'real witches' can be Christian, Jewish, Pagan or of any faith. The technology of witchcraft is pan-religion. Witches of the old school would have used the dominant faith at the time as a lens, whilst also practising witchcraft techniques. For example, Catholics might have worked with the Virgin Mary or Jesus alongside the spirits of place (*genii loci*) and the horned god and so on. Witchcraft and magic are the same thing. If you are in the sticks and need to find where to sink a well or what is wrong with your cow, none of these distinctions is important. Having the sixth sense will tell you where it is safe to eat, sleep or drink. That is the root of psychic ability. It is about getting on, survival, providing for your family and getting your daughters married off. So 'low' magic is really the most spiritual thing you can do. By turning to powers which are innate in and around you to improve the lot of your family and community, you are changing and evolving. Incidentally, this is why it was a mistake when British magic became enthralled by Eastern culture in the nineteenth and early-twentieth centuries. Rather than low magic and practical sorcery, people such as Dion Fortune advocated meditation to improve yourself. However, psychology and magic are not the same thing.

There isn't one right way to do magic, there are many right ways. Whether it is running a bath, saying prayers by candlelight, praying at your altar, lighting incense, calling in the deities or ancestral spirits you are working with or casting a spell or charm at the right hour of the right day — all of these build towards success because they are telling you that you are doing it correctly. They are mental gymnastics as well as proper energies in their own right. Real, but also a way of convincing yourself that it is real. Equally, you could go out in your car and drive to a certain tree and just sit beside it and get exactly the same result as someone doing all that ritual magic. For you, that tree is the gateway. We each need a method, whatever works for us. The second part of being successful is, once you've done the magic, not to look back, not to look over it, mull it over or worry about it. You can't interfere with it.

Everyone is hard wired for clairvoyance and the psychic as well as magic. I would argue that the reason we are sitting here today is because our ancestors were skilled at magic. That is why we didn't get eaten by sabre-toothed tigers, fall down a well or eat poisoned food. There are two kinds of magician in the world: the magician who says 'This is an interesting adventure...' and the magician who cannot wait to get out of here. A successful magician needs to tap into the art of play. Our ancestors used artwork. They drew the animals they liked to eat. There are marks in the stone where they threw their spears at the painted animals. This was to make sure they would drive the real animal into their spears. Play — pick up a piece of string and tie a knot in it so whatever you desire you have knotted and is now yours. Or pick a herb that seems to correspond with how you are feeling. Work with it. The object embodies your intention. It is about re-enacting what you want, about creation. Magic is at the root of our modern drama. Fake it until you make it.

A note on Power Places

(relating to Isla's Yew trees, Forest's land-based work, Eliana's journey to Wayland's Smithy, David's to Lullover Hill and Ffyona's plant and hunter-gatherer locations.)

Certain places in nature have the capacity to help humans enter an altered state of awareness or impart powerful medicine. It is a common pattern in transcendental experiences to be drawn to a place as if guided. If we surrender to this magnetic pull, something 'triggers' our mindset into a new or expanded dimension of consciousness in which normal time-space references cease to exist. When consciousness returns to normal, a new and more meaningful paradigm has become integrated within us. Sacred power places are said to maintain the overall health of our planet and to transmit and receive energy encoded with information. Indigenous minds say these places must be honoured and respected. In many cultures a tradition of reciprocity (leaving offerings at a sacred site) is considered integral to a positive result.

Up to 150 earth chakras have been located on the Earth's surface – on ocean beds, mountain peaks, flatlands and valleys. Others believe the chakra locations lie deep inside the Earth, not on the surface of the tectonic plates. These energy centres are thought to have different functions, representing feminine and masculine energies[12] as well as positive, negative or neutral energy. An ancient pilgrimage route follows the European 'spine' chakras from Santiago de Compostella in Spain to Roslyn in Scotland via Toulouse, Orleans, Chartres, Paris and Amiens. In Britain, legends cling to the Spine of Albion.

Chartres Cathedral in France is reported to be the heart chakra on the old pilgrimage route from Santiago de Compostella to the North of Scotland. It was built in silence, in gratitude to the Black Madonna – a statue or painting of the Virgin Mary in which she and Jesus are depicted with dark skin – and has a magnificent labyrinth. The cathedral was founded as a Mystery School 1,000 years ago. It was there that St. Bernard of Clarvioux combined the visionary teachings of Plato with Christian mysticism and introduced the seven Liberal Arts. In Southern Ireland, the hill of Uisneach holds Ail na Mireann (the stone of divisions) under which lies Éiru, the sovereignty goddess, after whom the country was named.

12. *Locations associated with the Earth's masculine chakra / ch'ama system include Mount Shasta in California, Lake Titicaca in Peru and Bolivia, Uluru or Ayres Rock in Australia, Glastonbury and Shaftesbury in England, the Great Pyramids near Mount Sinai and the Mount of Olives in Jerusalem, a roving or moving chakra in Western Europe and Mount Kallas and the Himalayas in Tibet. Those associated with the feminine chakra / ch'ama system include Aconcagua in Argentina, Lake Titicaca in Peru and Bolivia, Qosqo and Chavin de Huantar in Peru, the Putumayo district in Colombia, Chichen Itza in the Yucatan and Teotihuacan in Mexico.*

As the Axis Mundi and the navel of Ireland, it marks the centre where the provinces came together. Uisneach is also linked with the Sun God Lugh who is said to have drowned in a lake on the hill and rests beneath an adjoining tumulus. On Beltane, a fire is lit on Uisneach each year to celebrate the coming of summer.

Our ancient landscape (including its megalithic constructions, stone circles, holy wells, sacred groves and medieval abbeys) reflects the lore of our lands. Just as a person, animal or bird has its own memory, consciousness and frequency, so does a sacred site or building. It is easy to forget that these had practical uses. After all, pyramids were used to enhance early seed germination and encourage uniformity of growth, aiding pollination. Obelisks resonate with, and focus, magnetic energy almost like antennae, whilst the ancient round towers in Ireland are said to be powerful amplifiers for alpha brainwaves which are known to positively affect human consciousness.

Our landscape contains a matrix of energies comprising both underground watercourses and an over-ground network. Sacred sites are the distribution centres that collect earth energies. Typically, a high density of energies – Ley lines – converge at each site. Node-points in each energy system represent the five elements – fire, wood, water, earth and metal. In Somerset, in South West England, for example, the ancient fire beacon at Corton Denham represents fire, a lone tree on Burrow Hill is wood, Chalice Well in Glastonbury constitutes water and the long barrow at Stoney Littleton is earth. Metal might be represented by the steel mast above the city of Wells. The standing stones at The Cove and stone circles at Stanton Drew are like acupuncture needles in the meridians and acupuncture points of the Earth.

Sacred monuments are usually built in places with a concentration of electromagnetic energies.[13] Often situated above subterranean geological structures that generate a natural electrical ground current, the location (usually atop a mound or hill), building or structure alignment (often eight degrees west of today's magnetic North), type of structure (whether a pyramid or ditch dug to a minimum of three feet deep), ore type (quartz, pure gold, copper are the best conductors), radioactive minerals (such as iron meteorite and granite) and ground are all important. Ground with lots of metal or water conducts telluric[14] currents. Ancient cultures in

13. *The Dragon Project Trust (DPT) was founded in 1977 to investigate the idea that prehistoric sites had unusual forces or energies associated with them. They found that the locations favoured by megalith builders tended to have a higher than average incidence of magnetic and radiation anomalies.*

14. *Of the soil.*

both the Northern and Southern hemispheres appear to have understood the resonance between Earth locations and different celestial bodies. The location of sacred buildings often mirrors the position of stars in the sky at important times in the wheel of the year, in particular equinoxes and solstices.

Common geomagnetic design principles include geometric forms – pyramids, cubes and circles – to harness the Earth's magnetic energy. The three-fold geo-spiral energy patterns of underground water were integrated into sacred sites, pyramids and walled cities. At Stonehenge the altar stone is set above a seven-coil spiral of springs and the heel stone above a forty-nine-coil spiral. It is said that on a fine frosty morning each stone transmits aerial energies to the other stones around it. The big stones carry an enormous electrical charge. It would take a huge quartz crystal to inhibit their transmission and absorb the message of the stones. Small pits found in the ground are located precisely where the rushing telluric current concentrates.

A note on the Felt Sense

(relating to Isla's communication with trees, Tim, Forest, Eliana and Davids' work on the land, Livvy's work with horses, Chloë's singing and Ffyona's work with plants.)

The felt sense is about embodiment. Or rather, bringing awareness inside the body. It moves our focus from actions and things to qualities of our internal experience. As opposed to behaving like machines, we become self-regulating organisms. Our heart is the key to experiencing the felt sense. It acts as an organ of perception, along with the gastro-intestinal tract and brain. Its electromagnetic field is sixty times greater, and its magnetic component approximately 5,000 times stronger than the brain. When the heart's magnetic field is in close proximity to the magnetic field of another person, animal, rock or plant, they synchronise to exchange information. This information is decoded by our hippocampus to provide us with a map of experience or a map of meanings.

We feel this exchange of information emotionally. Our field of frequencies is ordered and coherent when we feel emotions such as love and compassion, and disordered when we feel emotions such as anger or frustration. These frequencies are broadcast like radio waves. New emotions can alter the form of the electromagnetic field, and embed themselves as new communications that then affect our physiology. At the same time as we communicate with other organisms, the world takes or breathes us in as well. Experiencing this soul-essence sharing, we realise we are not alone. Our awareness of heart-encoded information is dependent on variables such as our schooling, previous relationships, environment and emotional experiences.

To experience the felt sense requires a person to be quiet and receptive, so that no thought or word interferes. It requires them to examine something that attracts their attention, noticing shapes, colours and how it feels. The eyes become soft-focused with increased peripheral vision. There is a shift in cardiac function. For deep intimacy and dialogue, the other organism should be treated with respect and asked for help. If we allow communications from other living organisms to flow through us, we feel subtle levels of movement in our bodies that we ordinarily neglect, anchoring the connection in our experiences. When we pay attention at this level, wonderful things happen. Heart-focused techniques increase intuitive awareness and efficient decision-making. Dissociation and hyper-vigilance are both counter-acted.

Practitioner contact details

Isla Macleod   islajmacleod@gmail.com

Tim Raven   timravenHarp@gmail.com

Forest Melinn   dumnoniiwytch@gmail.com

Eliana Harvey   www.shamanka.com

Livvy Adams   www.paintedhorse.org.uk

Chloë Goodchild   www.thenakedvoice.com

Ffyona Campbell   www.wildfoodwalks.co.uk

Mark Ovland   www.freelygivenretreats.org

The practitioners in this book are based in, or have strong work connections with, the South West of England.

England

London

Bristol

Glastonbury

Holwell

Buckfastleigh

Bibliography

Beth, R. (2008). *The Green Hedge Witch. A guide to wild magic.* Robert Hale.

Buhner, S. H. (2014). *Plant Intelligence and the Imaginal Realm.* Bear & Company.

Buhner, S. H. (2004). *The Secret Teachings of Plants. In the direct perception of nature.* Bear & Company.

Campbell, F. (2012). *The Hunter-Gatherer Way. Putting Back the Apple.* Wild Publishing.

Corbin, N. M. (2008). *Weather Shamanism.* Bear & Company.

D'Angelo, J. (2005). *The Healing Power of the Human Voice. Mantras, Chants, and seed Sounds for Health and Harmony.* Healing Arts Press.

Dawson, K. & Allenby, K.D. (2010). *Matrix reinprinting using EFT. Rewrite your past, transform your future.* Hay House

Dieu-Le-Veut, A. *92016) Reclaiming Sovereignty.*

Druce, C. *(2015) Stonehenge Experience. A guide through millennia of building monument and legend.*

Farmer, S. (2006). *Animal Spirit Guides. An easy-to-use handbook for identifying and understanding your power animals and animal spirit helpers.* Hay House.

Fortune, D. (2000). *Glastonbury Avalon of the Heart.* Weiser Books.

Gerber, R. (2000). *A Practical Guide to Vibrational Medicine. Energy Healing and Spiritual Transformation.* William Morrow, an imprint of HarperCollins Publishers

Giono, J. (1995). *The Man who Planted Trees.* The Harvill Press.

Goodchild, C. *(2015) The Naked Voice.* North Atlantic Books.

Graves, T. (1978). *Needles of Stone.* Turnstone Press Ltd.

Greene, J. S.B. (2009). *The Mythic Tarot.* Random House.

Groom, N. (2013). *The Seasons. A celebration of the English Year.* Atlantic Books.

Halberg, J. B. (2005). *Seed of Knowledge Stone of Plenty. Understanding the lost technology of the ancient megalith-builders.* Council Oak Books.

Harari, Y. N. (2011). *Sapiens. A brief History of Humankind.* Vintage Books.

Harvey, C.G. (2007). *The New Encyclopaedia of Flower Remedies. The definitive practical guide to all flower remedies, their making and use.* Watkins Publishing.

Heath, R. (2005). *Powerpoints. Secret rulers & hidden forces in the landscape.* Bluestone Press.

Howard, M. (1995). *The Sacred Ring. The pagan origins of British folk festivals and customs.* Capall Bann Publishing.

Johnson, D. H. (1992). *Body. Recovering our Sensual Wisdom.* North Atlantic Books.

Kaye, T. (Composer) (2014). *Brotherhood with Trees: Descriptions forming a meditative pathway to reconnect.* [T. Kaye, Performer]

Kindred, G. (2014). *Sacred Earth Celebrations.* Permanent Publications.

Levine, P. A. (1997). *Waking the Tiger. Healing trauma.* North Atlantic Books.

Mate, G. (2003). *When the Body Says No.* Vintage Canada.

Matthews, J. (2001). *The Celtic Shaman. A practical guide.* Rider.

McKusick, E. D. (2014). *Tuning the Human Biofield.* Healing Arts Press.

Pogacnik, M. (1997). *Nature Spirits & Elemental Beings. Working with the Intelligence in Nature.*

Findhorn Press.

Roberts, A. (Editor) (1978). *Glastonbury Ancient Avalon, New Jerusalem.* Rider.

Rutherford, L. (2008). *The View Through the Medicine Wheel. Shamanic Maps of how the universe works.* John Hunt Publishing.

Swan, J. A. (1990). *Sacred Places. How the Living Earth seeks our Friendship.* Bear & Company.

Taylor, K. (2012). *Celestial Geometry. Understanding the Astronomical Meanings of Ancient Sites.* Watkins Publishing.

Trauma-Informed Care in Behavioral Health Services. Treatment Improvement Protocol (TIP) Series, No. 57. Center for Substance Abuse Treatment (US). Rockville (MD): Substance Abuse and Mental Health Services Administration (US); 2014.

Queally, J. (2017). *Reconnecting with Celtic Trees.* Earthwise Publications.

With Thanks

Big thanks to Matt Bryden for his wonderful editing job. Also to Fulvio Naselli and Ian Stewart for bringing my photographs alive and to Blossom Chambers for her help with design.

Thanks to my teachers, the eight wonderful practitioners who contributed to this book. To Mark for his Dharma teachings and to David, chapter 5 for contributions to the introduction and notes section.

Thanks to the following course providers and facilities during my year of awakening: Awaken the Language of the Heart *(Hawkwood College) with Wilhelmina Swindell and Tobias Kaye;* Resonance: Unlocking the Healing Power of the Voice *(Hawkwood College) with James D'Angelo;* Aromatherapy Product Making *and* Manifesting with the Moon *courses with Sara Turner (Essentially Flowers, online);* Dowsing Professionally Level 1 *(The Avebury School of Esoteric Studies) with Maria Wheatley;* Rune Introduction *with Rosemary Taylor;* EFT and Matrix re-imprinting *with Karl Dawson;* Shaman's journey and Spirits of Nature *courses (Schumacher College & Åsbacka, Sweden) with Jonathan Horwitz and Zara Waldback;* Tuning forks & Orions Gate workshops *(Suara Sound Academy) with Debbi Walker;* Storytelling *with Paul & Clare Jackson;* Connecting with Elementals *(The Burren, County Clare, Ireland) with Marko Pogacnik and organised by Jackie Queally;* Seaweed & Seashore & Berries and Nuts, Roots, Lichens & Fungi *Wild Food Walks (East Prawle and The Dart river) with Ffyona Campbell;* Astroshamanism *(Shamanka) with Celina Marshall and* Medicine Wheel *with Tim Raven.*

Many thanks to Rosemary Taylor for a series of powerful shamanic healings and my first energetic release.

Thanks to all my family and good friends and to the people I met throughout the year, and particularly to Kevin Jones for his ongoing love and support.

Lastly, thank you to my mum for drawing the images on the front cover. Apple helps us to contact our higher purpose and to channel our energies in the right direction. It develops the heart.

All profit earned from the publication of *Enchanted Beings* will be donated towards the purchase of a plot of land. The author has a vision of 25 acres of wild food, forest and clean water where a community of like-minded practitioners can live and undertake workshops, healings and teachings.

Author

Jenny Chapman practised for thirty five
years as a Rehabilitation Counsellor helping
people return to work after accident, illness
and injury. In 2012, she re-trained at the
Shamanka school of shamanic training
for women, since when she has attended a
range of specialized courses to assist her own
shamanic practice.

Jenny was born in a farming community and
lives in Somerset, South West England. She is
familiar with animal husbandry and the cycles
of the land that echo the human condition
– when best to plant, grow, harvest and die
back.

Throughout her life Jenny has travelled extensively, often working with
indigenous cultures and people to better understand their healing,
initiation and ceremonial techniques. In 2014, she travelled with a master
shaman across South and Central America, visiting the seven *ch'amas*. Jenny
is a published author and part one of the *Two White Feathers* trilogy is based
on this pilgrimage.

Enchanted Beings is the second book in the *Two White Feathers* trilogy.

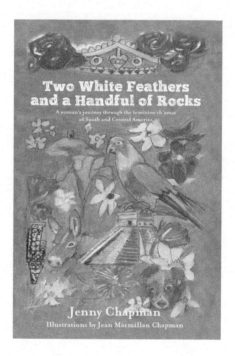

For further information please visit.

www.twowhitefeathers.com